THE NATIVE MARKET
of the
Spanish New Mexican Craftsmen
1933–1940

THE NATIVE MARKET
of the
Spanish New Mexican Craftsmen
1933–1940

by
Sarah Nestor

Revised Edition
with a
New Foreword
by
George B. Paloheimo

SOUTHWEST HERITAGE SERIES

SUNSTONE PRESS

SANTA FE

Sunstone books may be purchased for educational, business, or sales promotional use.
For information please write: Special Markets Department, Sunstone Press,
P.O. Box 2321, Santa Fe, New Mexico 87504-2321.

Library of Congress Cataloging-in-Publication Data

Nestor, Sarah, 1943-
The native market of the Spanish New Mexican craftsmen, 1933-1940 / by Sarah
Nestor ; new foreword by George B. Paloheimo.
    p. cm. -- (Southwest heritage series)
Includes index.
ISBN 978-0-86534-734-2 (softcover : alk. paper)
1. Native Market, Santa Fe, N.M. 2. Markets--New Mexico--Santa Fe. 3. Handicraft-
-New Mexico--Santa Fe--Marketing. I. Title.
HF5472.U7S266 2009
381'.4574550978956--dc22
                            2009033285

Published in

WWW.SUNSTONEPRESS.COM
SUNSTONE PRESS / POST OFFICE BOX 2321 / SANTA FE, NM 87504-2321 /USA
(505) 988-4418 / ORDERS ONLY (800) 243-5644 / FAX (505) 988-1025

The Southwest Heritage Series is dedicated to Jody Ellis and Marcia Muth Miller, the founders of Sunstone Press, whose original purpose and vision continues to inspire and motivate our publications.

CONTENTS

SOUTHWEST HERITAGE SERIES

I

THE SOUTHWEST HERITAGE SERIES

"The past is not dead. In fact, it's not even past."
—William Faulkner, *Requiem for a Nun*

The history of the United States is written in hundreds of regional histories and literary works. Those letters, essays, memoirs, biographies and even collections of fiction are often first-hand accounts by people who wanted to memorialize an event, a person or simply record for posterity the concerns and issues of the times. Many of these accounts have been lost, destroyed or overlooked. Some are in private or public collections but deemed to be in too fragile condition to permit handling by contemporary readers and researchers.

However, now with the application of twenty-first century technology, nineteenth and twentieth century material can be reprinted and made accessible to the general public. These early writings are the DNA of our history and culture and are essential to understanding the present in terms of the past.

The Southwest Heritage Series is a form of literary preservation. Heritage by definition implies legacy and these early works are our legacy from those who have gone before us. To properly present and preserve that legacy, no changes in style or contents have been made. The material reprinted stands on its own as it first appeared. The point of view is that of the author and the era in which he or she lived. We would not expect photographs of people from the past to be re-imaged with modern clothes, hair styles and backgrounds. We should not, therefore, expect their ideas and personal philosophies to reflect our modern concepts.

Remember, reading their words and sharing their thoughts is a passport back into understanding how the past was shaped and how it influenced today's world.

Our hope is that new access to these older books will provide readers with a challenging and exciting experience.

II

FOREWORD TO THIS EDITION
by
George B. Paloheimo

When reflecting on the remarkable woman who was my mother, Leonora Curtin Paloheimo, I found it hard to keep from going into hyperbole. Cut from the same cloth as her grandmother, Eva Scott Fenyes, and mother, Leonora Scott Muse Curtin, she had a combination of talents inherited from both. She was a gifted artist, as was her grandmother, a creative writer (her letters were written with a rare combination of style and grace, and her command of the English language was exceptional), a shrewd business woman, and as warm and gracious a hostess as one could ever hope to meet.

All three women also had a passion for history, preservation and art, be it archeological, ethnic or regional. Mother never pursued her talent as a watercolorist, beyond painting for pleasure, but I'm sure if she had, she would have been successful. She did publish a small book of poetry, entitled *Gallant Sprouts*, and often wrote poetry as a form of relaxation.

Above all, Leonora Curtin Paloheimo was a warm, loving and concerned individual, as demonstrated by her and her husband's adopting four Finnish orphans in the late 1940s, embracing the task of motherhood with enthusiasm and devotion.

This same generosity of spirit and determination to help is what was invaluable to her in the formation of Native Market. Possessed of the same spine of steel as her mother and grandmother, she was undaunted as she overcame the many obstacles she faced in her endeavors. That determination, combined with charm and guile, is what brought her dream of an outlet for New Mexican artists, trained in local arts and crafts, to sell their wares, a reality. Recognizing that these skills were rapidly disappearing, she was instrumental in creating training programs through the WPA, thus helping to save these traditions for the future, as shown by the success of the modern day Spanish Market in Santa Fe.

Her contributions to the cultural landscape of Santa Fe and northern New Mexico were not limited to the Native Market. She was, along with her mother, a founding member of the Spanish Colonial Arts Society and a major contributor to the Museum of Spanish Colonial Arts, where the gift shop bears her name. She was also a board member and a major donor to the School of American Research, now known as the School of Advanced Research.

Her generosity to cultural and educational endeavors extended far beyond Santa Fe. Personal and Paloheimo Foundation donations of various types were made to the Southwest Museum in Highland Park, Pasadena, Finlandia University in Hancock, Michigan, and the Finlandia Foundation. Her grandmother's mansion in Pasadena, California, is now part of the Pasadena Historical Museum. Fully furnished as it was at the turn of the 20th century, this house museum is the only one still open to the public showing the elegant lifestyle of that era in Pasadena. In Finland, her husband's family estate is now home of the Sibelius Academy. The Academy's alumni are spread throughout the world, and support by way of grants continues this day through the Paloheimo Foundation.

El Rancho de las Golondrinas is perhaps her most enduring legacy. This living history museum, depicting Spanish Colonial life in New Mexico, was the result of a multi-year collaborative effort by her and her husband, Y.A. Paloheimo. It is the only one of its kind in the state of New Mexico, and is a lasting monument to both of them.

I hope you enjoy reading this account of the Native Market, and Leonora Curtin Paloheimo's part in it, and thus gain an appreciation for the person she was.

III

REVISED EDITION

The Native Market
of the
Spanish New Mexican Craftsmen
1933–1940

Revised Edition

A. El Parian Analco, home of the Native Market, 1937 – 1940. Rendering by Bill Lumpkins, August, 1937.

Contents

Foreword

Some of my earliest memories of the movement for the preservation of historical Santa Fe architecture are associated with the Curtin family. One of the most vivid of these recollections is a conversation I had with Leonora Paloheimo's grandmother, Mrs. Feynes, in the late 1920s. She received me very ceremoniously lying on her couch, in her house on the Acequia Madre. The purpose of my visit was to solicit funds for the preservation of the historic style of architecture in Santa Fe. In this I was successful for she was very generous and deeply interested in the efforts being made for the preservation of Santa Fe's historic architecture.

Leonora is still carrying on the architectural preservation tradition by the wonderful work she and her husband George are doing in the restoration of El Rancho de las Golondrinas in La Cienega where they are creating a museum of Spanish colonial life in New Mexico.

The Native Market described so vividly and well in the following pages was as influential in the preservation and development of the native Spanish American crafts as the reconstruction of the portal of the Palace of the Governors had been in the development of the Santa Fe style of architecture in New Mexico.

John Gaw Meem
Santa Fe, 1978

Preface

When I was approached by the Colonial New Mexico Historical Foundation over a year ago with the idea of writing a book on the Native Market, I was shown two old albums. They contained newspaper clippings, advertisements and financial records from the Native Market, some unpublished notes about the Market written by Leonora Paloheimo, and old photographs of the Market and its crafts. In addition to these fascinating materials, interviews with the following people have made this book possible: Margaret Baca DeValle, Carmen Espinoza, Virginia Hunter Ewing, Gladys Gilmore, Concha Ortiz y Pino de Kleven, Abad Lucero, Bill Lumpkins, Janette Lumpkins, Wayne Mauzy, Preston McCrossen, Dorothy McKibbin, Dolores Perrault Montoya, Leonora Paloheimo, Pedro Quintana, Alice Rossin, David Salazar, and Brice Sewell.

In addition I would like to thank Leonora Paloheimo, Ann Vedder, Alan Vedder, Christine Mather, and Marc Simmons for reading over the manuscript and offering many helpful suggestions. Thanks are also due to Charlene Cerny and Nora Fisher for their comments on textiles, to Sylvia Loomis and Richard Eng for helping to locate crafts for additional photographs which were taken, and to the Museum of New Mexico Photo Archives for the use of photographs from their files. I am also indebted to Gene F. Doyle's article, "Santa Fe's 'Original Old Curio

Store,' " which appears in *The Denver Westerners Brand Book,* Volume 24, for information on the Candelario store. Finally, thanks are due to George (Y.A.) Paloheimo, who first inspired the idea for the book, gathered the original materials together, and has shepherded the manuscript with care and helpfulness through to its publication.

Sarah Nestor
Santa Fe, 1978

1. Introduction

Anglo-Americans in New Mexico were a major cause of the decline of traditional Spanish New Mexican crafts in the nineteenth century; in a reverse swing, they helped to bring about a revival in the twentieth century. When the railroad came west in the 1880s life in New Mexico changed almost overnight, and crafts which had thrived in isolation declined rapidly. Then in the 1920s and 1930s artists, anthropologists, educators, and other patrons in the state, recognizing the unique beauty and charm of New Mexico's Spanish colonial crafts, saw the need not only to preserve crafts from the past, but also to encourage their revival in the present. Santa Fe's "Native Market" of the 1930s, with Anglo-American support and a tremendous surge of diligence and creativity on the part of Spanish New Mexican craftsmen, played an important part in that revival.

The Native Market provided a sales outlet for the craftsmen, first in a shop on Palace Avenue from 1934 to 1937, and then in expanded quarters on College Street from 1937 to the middle of 1940. In addition, working closely with a training program for craftsmen in vocational schools throughout the state during those years, the Market offered guidance in the design of high quality, traditional New Mexican crafts. Designs were adapted for contemporary living when it seemed necessary, and craftsmen were also encouraged to experiment within the tradition.

The extant crafts of eighteenth through mid-nineteenth century New Mexico upon which twentieth century revival crafts were based— furniture, textiles, religious art—reflect the rugged and isolated life of the people who made them. Colonists who first came from Mexico and Spain to New Mexico in 1598 left a country which was still essentially medieval. This was particularly true of the rural Spanish villages from which some of the early colonists emigrated. The Renaissance, baroque, and neo-classic styles which subsequently swept across Europe to Spain had a long way to travel to Mexico and then north to the remote New World colony.

The colonists, who lost all their goods and fled to Mexico during the Pueblo Revolt of 1680, certainly saw post-medieval styles before they returned to New Mexico in 1692. And objects like the occasional religious images brought north from Mexico exerted some influence on local *santeros* (saint makers). But in short, any influences upon New Mexican colonial crafts came through Mexico until the opening of the Santa Fe Trail in 1821. Furthermore, Spain did not allow any of her colonies, including Mexico, to trade with non-Spanish countries.

New Mexico gained some contact with the non-Spanish world when foreign goods became available at the annual fair licensed in Chihuahua in 1805, and especially after Mexican Independence in 1821. New Mexicans attended the fair to barter sheep, hides, and blankets for long sought-after luxuries like fine clothing, religious books and medals, porcelain dishes, and Chinese leather chests. After the first quarter of the nineteenth century Directory and especially Empire influence can be seen in some New Mexican daybeds and chairs. Calico, coarse muslin, and finespun woolen Manchester cloth appeared in New Mexico. But still, it was an arduous journey over either the Chihuahua or the Santa Fe Trail.

Forced to rely upon early Spanish traditions and the imagery and patterns of those objects which travelled north from Mexico, or, after 1821, over the Santa Fe Trail, the New Mexico colonists, left to their own devices and materials, evolved a style of their own. Native dyes and pigments were adopted. Animal hides and gessoed wood were used in place of canvas for painting. Sturdy, simple furniture was made of native pine, with minimal ironwork, and sometimes with carved relief or painted designs.

The isolation of New Mexican colonists, their struggle for survival in a harsh environment, and a decrease in tools supplied by the government did not encourage refinement in their crafts. The unique beauty of New Mexican crafts throughout the eighteenth and most of the nineteenth centuries lies in the simplicity and pleasing proportions of the furniture, the soft textures and rich earth tones of its weaving, the intensity of feeling to be found in its religious art, and in the charm of decorative elements present in all the crafts.

These qualities were an expression of the culture which produced them—but after the coming of the railroad and all it transported in the 1880s a self-consciousness, often a feeling of inadequacy, led to a decline in many aspects of the culture, including its crafts. With the importation of eastern furniture in quantities the traditional high *trastero* (cupboard) came to resemble the ubiquitous meat safe. New Mexican relief carving gave way to compassed geometric designs and Victorian-style applied wood decorations. New pieces from the East such as washstands, ironing tables, and beds were copied. Textile production deteriorated when the coarse wool of the Rambouillet sheep was substituted for the soft wool of the Merino sheep which the colonists had used.

Commercial dyes produced harsh colors in yarn and the introduction of cotton warps made for less durable fabrics. Mass-produced plaster saints and chromolithographic prints from the East partially replaced New Mexican *santos* (saints). Not only were Eastern styles (not necessarily inferior, but often incongruous) superimposed on traditional New Mexican crafts, but, perhaps more importantly, the quantity of mass-produced inferior objects replaced the quality of individually made crafts, with their careful workmanship, idiosyncracies, and charm.

It should also be mentioned that a new craft sprang up in nineteenth century New Mexico thanks to Anglo-American traders and soldiers. Discarded tin food containers and lard and lamp oil cans were salvaged, cut, and re-pieced by Spanish New Mexicans to make frames for images of saints, candleholders, and trinket boxes. Tin, with its sudden availability and malleability, became tremendously popular in New Mexico, where metal had always been scarce. Unfortunately tin work, too, had deteriorated as a craft by the end of the nineteenth century. Pieces were often cut in elaborate Victorian shapes and painted with red and green house paint decorations in place of earlier delicate stamped designs.

Then near the turn of the century certain far-sighted traders and curio dealers began to see the value of New Mexican Spanish crafts. The most famous store was the Candelario's Original Old Curio Store on San Francisco Street in Santa Fe, which had its origins in a general store and meat market owned by the Spanish New Mexican family in the late nineteenth century. The Candelario brothers appointed Jake Gold, "the forerunner of all curio dealers," as its manager in the 1880s. Gold added crafts and curios to the general merchandise, and named the store the Original Jake Gold Curio Store. The Candelarios

Candelario's Original Old Curio Store, Santa Fe, circa 1915-20. John Candelario is on the right. Photo by T. Harmon Parkhurst.

later named the store The Original Old Curio Store and dispensed with Gold's services in 1903, but they continued to barter supplies for New Mexico Indian and Spanish crafts. Families who came from rural areas to barter were housed and fed in the Candelario Compound adjoining the store, their burros lodged in a nearby yard in Burro Alley. As business expanded the store's goods were increased by the hiring of Indian, Spanish, and Mexican craftsmen to work on the spot. The Original Old Curio Store was the most fabulous store in the Southwest in its day, housing a vast array of junk and treasures.

And there were other stores. In 1902 H.C. Yontz opened a store on San Francisco Street in Santa Fe where he sold gold and silver filigree jewelry as well as other jewelry and Indian blankets. (Gold and silver filigree working was basically a Mexican rather than a New Mexican craft, but it was made in New Mexico from the 1870s, following the development of gold and silver mines in the state.) In 1915 Julius Gans opened his Southwest Arts and Crafts shop on the south side of the Santa Fe plaza. Essentially a factory, Gans' shop had silversmiths, weavers, and clothing manufacturers at work on the premises, and sold both New Mexican Indian and Spanish crafts.

Santa Fe crafts stores proliferated in the 1920s: shops like the Old Santa Fe Trading Post on Cathedral Place, the La Fonda shop, and the Spanish and Indian Trading Company (first in Prince Plaza, then north of La Fonda) collected and sold both Indian and Spanish New Mexican crafts. A scholarly interest in the crafts developed through the 1920s and 1930s, so that early collectors like Kenneth Chapman, Dr. Harry Mera, A.V. Kidder of Harvard's Peabody Museum, Sylvanus Morley, and Jesse Nusbaum often were to be seen in the alley behind the Spanish and Indian Trading Company in the early morning hours, inspecting goods as they arrived from nearby villages and pueblos.

It should be mentioned that in spite of "Progress" a few rural New Mexican villages and individuals had maintained a living crafts tradition. Most notable were Chimayo and villages near it, where weaving continued although commercial yarns and dyes were used, and Cordova, where José Dolores Lopez (1868-1938) and his descendants

José Dolores Lopez, the Cordova woodcarver, with some of his work.

carved *santos* and other objects from wood. Also, the *santero* Celso Gallegos of Agua Fria (1864-1943) filled his garden next to the Church of San Ysidro in Agua Fria with strange birds and animals as well as *santos* that he carved. He was inspired by a carving passed down through his family which, according to family legend, had been made by his great-great-grandfather in Mexico. Early patrons collected the works of these living craftsmen, as well as objects from earlier times.

By 1925 Concha Ortiz y Pino, with the encouragement of her father, José Ortiz y Pino, and the scholar Dr. Aurelio Espinoza, became interested in the colonial architecture and furniture of Galisteo, the isolated rural community south of Santa Fe where her family spent their summers. The residents appreciated her interest, and began to restore and preserve their homes as well as the church in Galisteo. This kindling of interest paved the way for the Colonial Hispanic Crafts School which she established in Galisteo in 1929. Traditional carding and spinning, natural dyeing of yarn and pelts, weaving, leatherworking, and furniture making were taught at the school, which also became a center for the revival of Spanish New Mexican folklore—dancing, singing, and storytelling. The school was run on the philosophy that students make objects first for wear, second for use in their homes, third for exchange among themselves, and only fourth for sale to stores and customers in Santa Fe.

Also, in 1925 a number of concerned artists, collectors, and other citizens in Santa Fe, led by Mary Austin and Frank Applegate, founded the Spanish Colonial Arts Society. A Spanish Colonial Arts Society pamphlet lists the original members, in addition to Mary Austin and Frank Applegate, as

> Mrs. Ruth Laughlin Alexander, Mr. and Mrs. A.S. Alvord, Mr. George Bloom, Mr. and Mrs. Gerald Cassidy, Dr. Kenneth Chapman, Miss Leonora Curtin, Mrs. Thomas Curtin, Senator Bronson M. Cutting, Mr. Andrew Dasburg, Mr. and Mrs. John DeHuff, Mrs. Charles H. Dietrich, Mrs. Lois Field, Mrs. William Field, Mrs. Alice Corbin Henderson, Mr. Wayne Mauzy, Mr. and Mrs. Cyrus McCormick, Mr. George McCrossen, Mr. Preston McCrossen, Mr. John Gaw Meem, Dr. Frank E. Mera, Mrs. Alice Clark Myers, Mr. Sheldon Parsons, Dr. Francis Proctor, Mrs. Marie Robinson, Mr. H. Cady Wells, Miss Mary C. Wheelwright, and others sensitive to Spanish culture.

Frank Applegate, an artist who had moved to Santa Fe in 1922, was an avid collector of Spanish colonial crafts. Mary Austin, a writer, had

Celso Gallegos, santero of Agua Fria. Photo by Ina Sizer Cassidy.

Crucifix by Celso Gallegos.
Photo by Art Taylor.

been hired by the Americanization Study of the Carnegie Foundation in 1918 to make a social and economic study of the Spanish-speaking population of New Mexico. She later reminisced in her autobiography, *Earth Horizon*, that "What I felt in New Mexico was the possibility of the reinstatement of the hand-craft culture and of the folk-drama, following the revival of those things in Mexico. I began definitely to plan to locate at Santa Fe and to work explicitly in that field."

The purpose of the Spanish Colonial Arts Society, Inc., as stated in its certificate of incorporation in 1929, was

> to encourage and promote Spanish Colonial Arts; to preserve and revive interest therein, to collect and display these arts and crafts, to promote and maintain suitable housing for such collections, to educate the public and the members of this corporation especially in the kind and qualities of the Spanish Colonial Arts and their meaning in the cultural life of Colonial times in New Mexico, and the relationship of other material from other Spanish colonies and from Spain as seen in the light of history and of art.

In addition to collecting and preserving old Spanish colonial crafts items in order to keep them within New Mexico, the Society encouraged the present-day revitalization of traditional Spanish crafts in the state. The first step, in 1925, was to sponsor a Spanish Market in the patio of the Museum of Fine Arts in conjunction with the Santa Fe Fiesta. The Market, which was held annually until 1932, offered the possibility of sales and prize money to any Spanish New Mexican craftsmen willing to produce traditional crafts.

As the knowledge of old designs and methods often lay dormant, members of the Society made drawings and took photographs of authentic Spanish colonial crafts in collections and showed them to any Spanish craftsmen or potential craftsmen who were interested. The Society cooperated particularly with the Normal School in El Rito and the county schools under Mrs. Otero Warren, which began to offer instruction in traditional Spanish crafts. Other Society projects included collecting and producing New Mexican folk dramas, and sponsoring the purchase of the Santuario de Chimayo (with funds supplied by Mary Austin and Frank Applegate), to be held in trust by the Archdiocese.

Because they realized that a year-round sales outlet for Spanish crafts was essential to revitalization, members of the Society opened a small shop in Sena Plaza in May, 1930. The Spanish Arts shop was managed by Mrs. Preston McCrossen, and then by Nellie Dunton until it closed in 1933. Although other Santa Fe shops had sold Spanish New Mexican as well as Indian crafts, The Spanish Arts was unique in its sale of Spanish New Mexican crafts exclusively, and in its support of present-day Spanish craftsmen in their production of authentic crafts. The shop bought and delivered materials to craftsmen in the villages, then bought the finished crafts from them and sold them at a small markup at the store. Wood carvings, furniture, tin work, and woven blankets were all successful sales items.

While the shop did succeed in attracting some attention in the West and on the East Coast, however, it was never a financial success, and depended for survival upon Mary Austin's support. Following the death of Frank Applegate and illness of Mary Austin (who died in 1934), the Society became inactive and the shop closed in 1933. This was a blow not only to patrons who were interested in New Mexican crafts, but especially to the craftsmen whose interest in their artistic heritage had been kindled once again, and whose livelihood in those Depression years often depended upon the income they had obtained from their crafts. Fortunately for all concerned, however, the Native Market opened its doors within six months of the closing of The Spanish Arts.

A corner of The Spanish Arts shop in Sena Plaza.

One of the rural vocational schools for crafts education started by Brice Sewell. Carding and Spinning Department is in the bottom row, Woodworking Department to the left, Tanning Department to the right, and Blacksmith Shop in the top row.

2. Palace Avenue

The impetus for the Native Market came from Miss Leonora Curtin,* who had been a member of the Spanish Colonial Arts Society. Reminiscing in 1968 about how she conceived the idea of the Market during the Depression, she recalled:

> I had returned to Santa Fe from the gloom enveloped East and I saw everywhere in the rural or village life of New Mexico, opportunities for the Spanish New Mexican people to help out their shrunken and meager economy by revival of of their old and traditional handicrafts.
>
> A convincing demonstration testifying to the worth of these resources had already been given by the Spanish Colonial Arts Society of Santa Fe in its small shop in Sena Plaza.
>
> Hard times and lack of adequate support forced the shop to close in 1933. But in a situation where no jobs were to be found, a skillful people, I knew, could surely help themselves and work at home on tasks that would yield the cash of which they stood in dire need.
>
> My enthusiasm rose quickly as the numerous possibilities unfolded, and ever mindful of the advantages in self respect that earning power offers over charitable or government aid, I made bold to speak out; I talked craft revival, teaching, marketing and every aspect to all who would listen.

It seemed essential to her not only that talented craftsmen have

---

*Miss Leonora Curtin, who later became Mrs. Y.A. Paloheimo, will generally be referred to as Miss Curtin or Leonora Curtin in the text, and as Mrs. Paloheimo when she is recollecting at a later date. Mrs. Paloheimo's mother's name was also Leonora Curtin. The only reference to her in the text is as Mrs. Thomas Curtin, in the list of members of the Spanish Colonial Arts Society in Chapter 1.

work, but also that adequate training be offered to potential craftsmen, training based upon examples of crafts from earlier times but with adaptations in style and color to make the objects saleable. Somehow, she felt,

> the traditional crafts would have to leap from the eighteenth and nineteenth century into the twentieth—but without loss of character. Appropriate examples of indigenous handmade articles from the past posed a difficult problem as collectors of antiques had already combed the country and about cleared it out, leaving nothing more Native than Montgomery Ward catalogues as a standard of excellence among the more remote villages and small farms.

During the course of her talk with local people Miss Curtin learned that Brice Sewell, who had been appointed State Director for Vocational Education and Training for New Mexico in 1932, was interested in training Spanish New Mexican craftsmen in their traditional crafts within the state's educational system. As early as 1930 El Rito Normal School had offered classes in weaving, furniture making, and iron working, but with state backing and funds Sewell planned to develop a state-wide system of crafts education in towns and rural communities.

The federal government also proved to be a source of funds for the new vocational program. The Smith-Hughes Act for the support of vocational training and rehabilitation programs, which was being utilized to help relieve nation-wide Depression unemployment, was generally used to train technicians such as machinists and welders. Fortunately, Sewell and Miss Curtin were able to persuade the program directors in Washington that the Spanish New Mexican crafts heritage was worthy of revival. The crafts amounted to much more than nick-nacks for roadside peddling; many Spanish people would prefer a trade that they could practice at home; and, furthermore, trained craftsmen would be an economic asset to the state. Thus, New Mexico became the first state to use federal funds for crafts education.

Sewell, who had previously taught in the Art Department at the University of New Mexico, hired four talented people, each with a special skill, to work with him in Santa Fe on the development and administration of the new vocational program. Henry Gonzales, a woodworker, became Sewell's right hand man. He was a trouble shooter, and

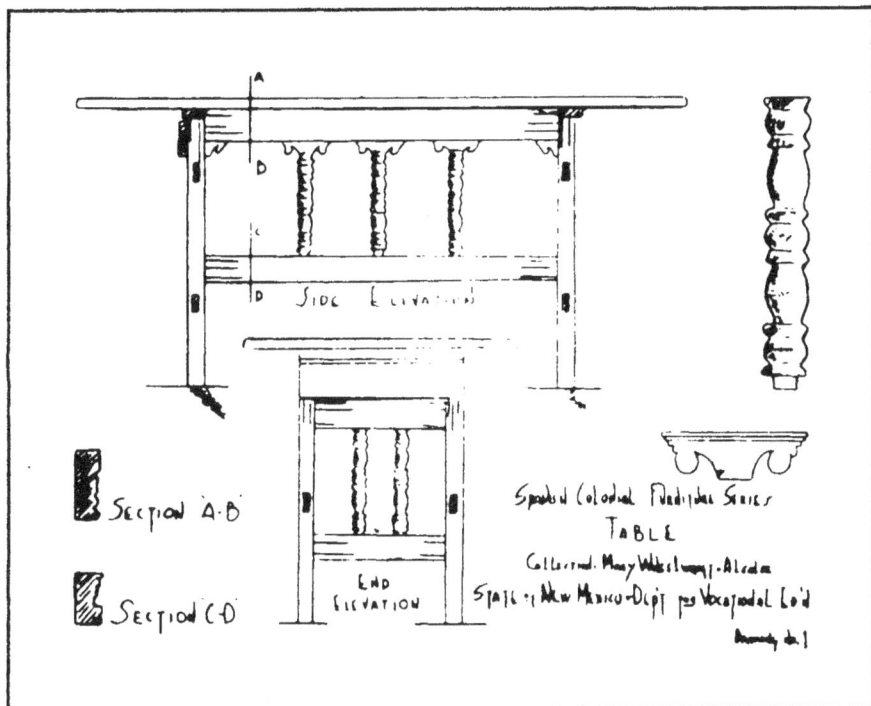

A page from the New Mexico Department for Vocational Education's "Bluebook" on woodwork and furniture. Photo by Art Taylor.

was sent ahead to set up new schools. Others on the staff were Bill Lumpkins, one of Sewell's art students at the university and a furniture maker; Dolores Perrault, a weaver and teacher; and Carmen Espinoza, a Spanish teacher and an authority on traditional Spanish culture. The dedicated group worked together for the next decade.

They decided that the basis of instruction would be a series of mimeographed books, with one volume devoted to each Spanish New Mexican craft to be taught. Each book would consist of scale drawings and instructions for making crafts pieces, as well as a preface containing general background information on the particular craft dealt with in that volume. Old crafts pieces from private collections were drawn by Carmen Espinoza and Bill Lumpkins, then the books were assembled, each person wrote the prefaces in his own area of expertise, and the books were blueprinted, or, later, xeroxed. The "Bluebooks," as they were called, are still cherished by craftsmen today. They included volumes on woodwork and furniture (Lumpkins), tinwork (Espinoza), painted chests (Sewell, Perrault, and Espinoza), *colcha* embroidery

(Espinoza and Perrault), vegetable dyeing (Perrault), tanning (Sewell), and even a volume on the construction of one-story houses. Although there was a volume on tinwork, it was never taught in the vocational schools because tinworking was still practiced by some families.

The next step was to persuade high schools in towns around the state to add crafts training to their vocational curriculums without disturbing the existing programs. The first crafts instructors for the schools, who were generally already teachers, were trained in Santa Fe. Later on, promising students sometimes became crafts instructors, and were sent to urban or rural schools around the state.

The key school was the Taos Vocational School, which, housed first in the Taos High School and then in its own building, was the largest school and had the most varied crafts curriculum. Early teachers at the Taos Vocational School included Mr. Manning, who made the program's first *trasteros*, chairs, and Taos beds (beds like couches with arms and slat backs); Leslie Cornish, the son of a Danish shipwright, and a skilled cabinet maker and patternmaker in wood himself; Mr. Arguello, who was a leather craftsman; and an instructor in weaving.

The first rural community school was started at Chupadero, twelve miles from Santa Fe, after eighty percent of the men in the village signed an agreement that they would cooperate. In a small remodelled adobe house instructors offered classes in tanning, wood-working, and weaving. The school was a great success in Chupadero, as the skills residents learned boosted the economy of the whole village. Chupadero residents had made a living for the last two hundred years hauling firewood from the mountains to Santa Fe on burros, but with the introduction of gas they had been forced to rely on their meager crops plus occasional odd jobs to survive.

Mrs. Paloheimo recalls that in an expression of gratitude for their vocational school and the Native Market the village of Chupadero once gave a *baile* (dance) for everyone connected with the enterprise. The evening of the *baile* was rainy and the steep dirt road to Chupadero was slick and precarious. When several carloads of guests from Santa Fe arrived at the schoolhouse there was no light, and no one about. The group decided to wait, however, and eventually two men appeared, a key was produced, and they were let into the school. The ensuing wait in the dark was somewhat eerie, but the patience of the group was am-ply rewarded when the men returned with light, more people, and guitars, and a joyful evening of folk dancing followed.

Men from Chupadero begin the twelve-mile walk to the Native Market in Santa Fe, their burros laden with tanned hides and woven goods.

Craftsmen of the Chupadero Vocational School with samples of their rawhide furniture.

The crafts building (above) and forge (below) at Rio en Medio Vocational School.

Other rural community schools for crafts education were opened when villages requested them, or when someone qualified showed interest in a particular town. Virginia Hunter Ewing recalls that in 1934 her husband Vernon Hunter, who was an art teacher and furniture maker, was on his way to Santa Fe to look for employment when he picked up a hitchhiker between Fort Sumner and Santa Rosa. The hitchhiker's destination was Puerto de Luna, south of Santa Rosa. Hunter was so enchanted by the little village that he proceded to Santa Fe and asked Sewell if he could start a vocational school in Puerto de Luna. With Sewell's approval and a guaranteed salary plus school expenses, Hunter returned to Puerto de Luna in the fall of 1934, rented the back of an old adobe house, and set up the school. Classes in furniture making, ceramics (with an instructor from Mexico), *colcha* embroidery, and a little tin work were offered to about twenty-five students, or a quarter of the population of Puerto de Luna. In the fall of 1935 Hunter accepted the job as Director of the WPA (Works Progress Administration) for New Mexico, so he left Puerto de Luna, and the school closed.

Schools were opened in remodelled or new buildings (designed by Bill Lumpkins) in such towns and villages as Limitar, Socorro, Abiquiu, Galisteo, San José, Grants, Roswell, Cienega, Puerto de Luna, Mora, Española, Santa Cruz, Costilla, Anton Chico, Agua Fria, Peñasco, Atarque, Cundiyo, Bernalillo, Portales, Los Lunas, Las Vegas (as part of Highlands University), and Taos, as well as Chupadero. Certain schools developed specialties: Chupadero became known for the rawhide and willow "Chupadero" style furniture which shows the influence of Mexican design (although correspondence with the Native Market shows that it was also made by Dan Ortiz at the Mora Vocational School); Abiquiu was primarily a tannery; and Cienega had furniture and pottery shops and a tannery.

Dolores Perrault Montoya recalls a strong family feeling and sense of dedication among the students, teachers, and staff in Santa Fe. Standards were high throughout the program. Design and craftsmanship were carefully supervised by instructors, with designs modified when it seemed practicable (for example, furniture dimensions were adjusted to modern needs). Students were guided toward ultimately designing for themselves. Remarkable though it may seem to us now, all students were also taught reading, writing, and arithmetic so that they could read the instructions in the "Bluebooks," and so they would be able to engage in business successfully later on.

Students from age sixteen were accepted at the school; only those who showed evidence of talent were allowed to stay. No tuition was charged, but students had to provide their own livelihood while they were at the school. Any income they did have generally came from the sale of crafts that they made to the Native Market, as the schools did not sell crafts directly to customers. Sewell recalls that many Taos Vocational School students were too poor to afford lodgings, so they slept on benches in the school and cooked in its fireplace. Taos residents raised funds for groceries for needy students by holding benefit dances and other social events. Training at the schools lasted about a year, until instructors felt that craftsmen were competent. When students were ready to go out on their own, their instructors tried to locate crafts jobs for them, or sometimes they returned home to produce crafts.

The survival of the craftsmen clearly depended upon an adequate sales outlet—and this was provided by the Native Market, which opened on Palace Avenue in Santa Fe on June 16, 1934. The Market, which was sponsored and subsidized by Miss Leonora Curtin, was to be run in a businesslike manner, in the hopes that both it and the craftsmen would eventually be able to stand on their own feet. Crafts were marked up only 33⅓ percent, to pay for the maintenance of the Market and salaries of craftsmen employed in the shop. Only crafts items which met a certain standard were bought by the Market, while other items were taken on consignment, but quality was always stressed. Mrs. Paloheimo later recalled,

> I realized that . . . the false stimulation of hopes would be a crime against the youth of the State, as the Vocational Schools and the Rehabilitation projects would be far reaching, and much of the training would depend on success or failure in the market. I therefore, in the Native Market, tried to discourage sentimentality and to uphold sound business principles.

In an attempt to create the most pleasant environment possible, the Native Market was housed in a light, commodious space. The walls were decorated with frescoes of scenes of Spanish New Mexican life which were painted by Bill Lumpkins. Once a visitor entered the store his senses were assaulted by homemade objects of all kinds. There were displays of carved furniture, handwoven blankets, tin framed mirrors, and wrought iron fixtures. Skeins of handspun yarn in many colors

Two vocational school scenes: spinning yarn (above) and tanning hides (below).

hung informally from racks; sets of furniture were displayed in alcoves; and weavers and spinners were employed to work continuously, demonstrating their craftsmanship to the public. A variety of smells arose from the leather goods and wood, and sometimes the air was filled with the sweet smell of the chamisa with which the dye was made. A shop for the finishing of village-made furniture was in the basement beneath the store. The central location of the Native Market, a block from the Santa Fe plaza, made it convenient for both residents and tourists.

The Native Market opened with a flourish. An article for the *Santa Fe New Mexican* (June 19, 1934) reported that "The market . . . did a rushing business its first day, selling out every finished chair and many other articles." Those articles included furniture (chairs, tables, beds, chests, *trasteros*, and doors); perishable foods as well as dried grains and vegetables; hides (calf, sheep, and goatskins, natural or tinted with vegetable dyes); parchments for lampshades and book bindings; rabbit skins; leather and horsehair reins, quirts, and sets for horses; hand spun and dyed yarns; wool blankets and both rag and wool rugs; *colcha* embroidery and drawn work on tablecloths and napkins; carved wooden trays, candlesticks, toys, *santos*, *nichos* (niches), smoking

Facade of the Palace Avenue Native Market.

Leather goods in the Native Market, including tanned hides, leather bound albums (on the stool), and reins, quirts, and sets for horses (hanging).

stands, buckles, and buttons; tin light fixtures, mirrors, picture frames, boxes, crosses, and flowerpots; and hand wrought iron locks, latches, hinges, door bolts, pokers, curtainrods, and candlesticks. Some of these objects, such as food, were dropped and new ones added as time went on.

Dolores Perrault was on loan from the vocational school program for 1934, to help set up the Native Market. She proved to be invaluable in selecting crafts for the store to purchase, and in dyeing yarn with vegetable dyes. She was succeeded by Pamela Parsons, Katherine C. Page, Eleanor Bedell, Roy Schoen, and Margaret Nelson as store managers between 1934 and the summer of 1937. Craftsmen employed at the Market included Tillie Gabaldon (dyeing and *colcha* embroidery), Deolinda Baca (*colcha* embroidery and some weaving), Doña Maria and her daughter Atocha Martinez (carding and spinning), Valentin Rivera, Margaret Baca, and David Salazar (weaving), Pedro Quintana (tinwork), David Lammlae (painting on tin, glass, and furniture), and David Villiaseñor from Mexico (woodcarving). Salazar recalls that David Lammlae, David Villiaseñor, and he were called the three Davids—big, little, and middle, respectively. In addition Abad Lucero, who made furniture in a back room of his home in Santa Fe, filled furniture orders for the Native Market. Village craftsmen who

Dolores Perrault (left), Doña Maria Martinez (center), and Atocha Martinez (right) demonstrate wool carding and spinning. Behind them hang skeins of yarn; to the left and in front are woven rugs and blankets of various kinds. Photo by T. Harmon

brought in their goods to the Native Market were given advice and instructions by these experts when they were needed.

Store managers also drove to outlying vocational schools and private homes in villages to pick up completed crafts, offer advice on techniques and designs, and deliver raw materials which were hard to get, such as tin, leather, and wool for hand spinning. Dorothy McKibbin, who worked for the Spanish and Indian Trading Company in the 1930s, remembers going with Eleanor Bedell to Chupadero with leather, Rio en Medio with tin, then continuing on to Truchas where hand-woven blankets and rag rugs were picked up and brought back to the Native Market.

The best wool for spinning could be obtained from the Navajo Reservation where a few long-strand fleeces were still to be found. Miss Curtin went to the Gallup area, where traders allowed her to open and hunt through mammoth wool sacks for the rare fleeces which could be hand carded and spun. The wool was hauled back to the Native Market in Santa Fe, and then issued to village spinners, who used the traditional *malacate*, or small spindle with attached weight, to spin the yarn. One of the best spinners was an old sheepherder from Atrisco (now a suburb of Albuquerque) who spun as he walked after his flock. He produced an unusually fine yarn without the help of even the simple *malacate.* Other spinners who wove at home included Pilar Trujillo, Adelaida Ortega, Juanita Jaramillo of Chimayo, F.R. Ortega of Anton Chico Vocational School, and Agnes Vigil of Mora.

A few older women who lived in Santa Fe came to the Native Market daily, gathered on the floor with piles of wool around them, and stayed to spin and gossip all day. One day a vigorous, middle-aged woman came to the Market from the village of Abiquiu to spin. She had great skill in spinning, which she had learned from her mother. (She confided to Miss Curtin that she had always blamed her mother for not teaching her anything valuable, but now she blessed her.) Everything went well for a time, but the resentment of the other women grew as she continually piled up more and better yarn than they, and consequently more earnings. One day the other women left in a group, having decided that she was a witch, and that they were very much afraid of her. They quite possibly knew that Abiquiu had had a tormenting problem of witchcraft since the nineteenth century. She was the only spinner at the Market for some time after that.

In 1935 Miss Curtin visited a large wool dealer in Boston and suc-

Native Market spinners. Doña Maria Martinez is in upper photograph, left; other spinners unidentified.

cessfully prevailed upon the management to ship small quantities of combed wool or "tops" to the Native Market. A fine grade of soft yarn could easily be spun from it, which was used for light weight blankets, in contrast to the coarser New Mexican wool, which was best suited to the weaving of rugs.

Textiles were initially most in demand at the Native Market. After fine to heavy wool or mohair was spun in villages, at the San José Training School, or at the Market, it was washed in amole root, which helped to retard moths. (Wool was not washed until after spinning because lanolin helped to hold it together while it was being spun.) Yarn was dyed at the Market using the traditional New Mexican natural dyes of indigo (blue, or green in mixture—imported), chamizo blanco (yellow), cañaigre root (gold-yellow), walnut hulls (brown), juniper bark (tan), brazilwood (henna-rose—imported), and cochineal (red—imported from Mexico). Black and white were natural, untreated colors. Alum and other mordants were used to make colors more permanent. The yarn, dyed in huge cauldrons in the back of the store, was sold to customers for knitting and weaving, and was also used for weaving and *colcha* embroidery done in the store.

Weaving in the Native Market was done on two regular treadle looms, one a two-and one a four-harness loom, plus one additional loom for extra orders. Woven fabrics were made primarily in 45-inch widths. The two-harness loom produced tapestry weave (Rio Grande blanket style), and the four-harness loom produced float weaves, which included diamond, whipcord, diagonal twill, partridge eye, herringbone, and houndstooth weaves. Traditional solid, striped, checked, and plaid patterns were woven. Upholsteries, draperies, blankets, rugs, and bedcovers were continually being woven on the premises, with thick all-white rugs an especially popular item.

David Salazar, who used the four-harness loom, recalls being taught to weave in his youth by an old man in La Cienega, a Mr. Rael. Salazar taught at the vocational school in Galisteo, then wove at the Native Market, primarily producing mohair draperies. In addition to textiles made at the Market, rugs and blankets were spun, dyed, and woven in such communities as Nambé, Taos, Española, Cordova, which produced all-white blankets, and Santa Rosa, where Manuel Tafoya wove plaid knee rugs. (Chimayo weavers were not represented at the Market because of their use of commercial dyes and yarns, but in any case they had other sales outlets.) Rag rugs, woven, braided, and

David Salazar at work.

hooked, were also sold at the Native Market, as were pillows made of rags woven through gunnysacks, although these were not made on the premises.

Colcha embroidery, which was done both in the Native Market and in villages, was used for pillow tops, chair seats, bedspreads, and borders on curtains. Workers in *colcha* employed motifs including traditional geometric designs, zigzagging bands of color, flowers and leaves, and animals such as lions, deer, and birds. *Colcha* embroidery is very fragile, but a number of old pieces which could be used as models at the Market and by village craftsmen were found in local collections. The *colcha* stitch, which was done at the Market with wool yarn on cotton ground, consists of solid parallel stitches, tacked down with short diagonal stitches. The embroidery may either solidly cover the ground fabric or be used in scattered designs over the white ground. Both types of *colcha* were done at the Native Market. English sheeting (heavy cotton twill) was ordered for *colcha* bedspreads and pillows, while Osenburg (coarse cotton with cottonseed) from Texas was used for *colcha* embroidered draperies.

Furniture was initially second in demand to textiles at the Native Market, although this was later reversed. All furniture was made of pine with mortise and tenon joints, the method of construction used in earlier times. Spindles were handmade without lathes. As in the past, pieces were often carved in relief with the background gouged away (with traditional Spanish design motifs such as lions, pomegranates, shells, and rosettes), or with scallops, "S" curves, chip carving, or grooves made with a plane. Furniture might be painted in the Market's finishing shop with similar traditional designs, or left with a natural finish.

Traditional styles were often modified for contemporary use, or traditional motifs were used on modern pieces. *Trasteros* were used as dining room pieces, but also, without interior shelves, as wardrobes. *Vargueños* (portable desks), which were made in Spain and Mexico but apparently not in colonial New Mexico, were made with matching tables at the Native Market, and were used as writing desks; larger desks were made as well. Beds, which were not seen in New Mexico un-

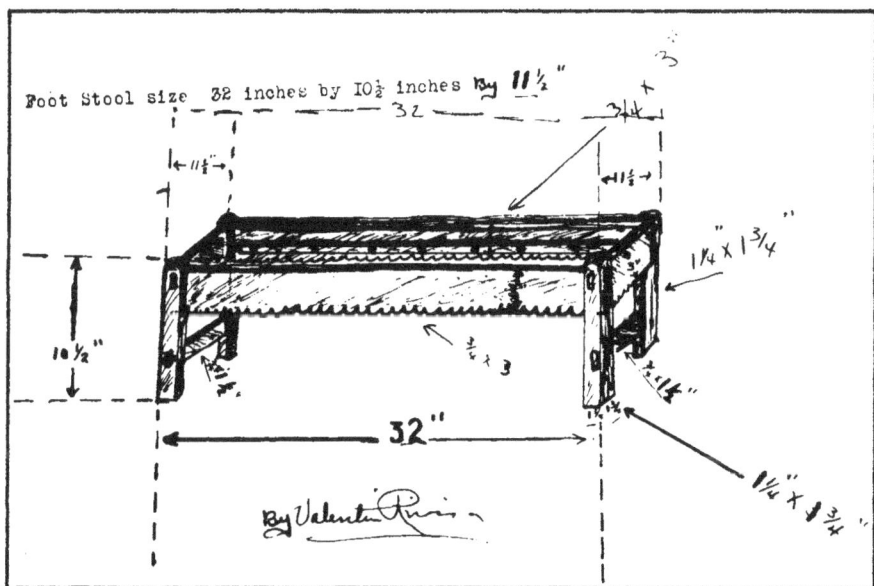

A typical working sketch for a foot stool to be made for the Native Market. Valentin Rivera's signature does not indicate that the weaver also made furniture, but that he took the customer's order. Photo by Art Taylor.

til the latter part of the nineteenth century, were most often made by the Market in twin-bed size, with carved Directory and Empire style head and foot boards. They were often accompanied by matching dressing tables, stools, chairs, or chests of drawers.

Chairs, with or without arms, were based on earlier colonial, Empire, and Directory styles. Unlike earlier pieces, Native Market chairs and stools had padded seats which were covered with *colcha* embroidery, handspun and woven fabric, or woven rawhide seats. Splat-backed couches or "Taos beds" bore more resemblance to church benches (though the couches were deeper) than to the daybeds introduced into New Mexico in the nineteenth century. Storage chests, with or without legs, were made in the traditional style. The Market chests were commonly used for storage of blankets or firewood, or as serving tables in dining rooms. *Alacenas* (wall cupboards) and *repisas* (hanging shelves) were based on traditional models. Traditional benches were also made, often for use on porches and portals. Coffee tables were often adaptations of the serving tables used in earlier times, and large dining room tables, which sometimes had matching backless ben-

Francisco Delgado, the tinsmith, at work in his living room at 503 Canyon Road, circa 1935. Photo by T. Harmon Parkhurst.

Pedro Quintana, tinsmith, surrounded by his work at the Native Market.

ches or chairs, were also often based upon earlier models. The rawhide and willow Chupadero chairs and tables were commonly used in patios or on portals.

Pedro Quintana worked full time at the Native Market filling orders for tinwork, and two other Santa Fe tinsmiths, Francisco Delgado and Francisco Sandoval, sold pieces to the Market. Tinwork included candle sconces, candelabras, lanterns, flowerpots, mirrors, picture frames, *nichos*, and ashtrays. Quintana, who began his career in 1916 as a filigree jeweler, remembers being asked by Sewell in 1933 to make a tin mirror frame like an old one in the collection of Pamela Parsons. Using cutters, chisel, hammer, and nails for stamping, he improvised; fortunately, his training as a jeweler stood him in good stead. A Frenchman named Frank Laurent who did sheet metal work taught him how to use solder. The expensive sheets of lead-coated rust proof tin which Quintana used were imported from West Virginia by the Market because of their mellow, pewter-like finish.

While furniture, textiles, and tinwork made up the bulk of the Native Market's crafts, ironwork (andirons, hinges, and locks) made by craftsmen Pablo Vigil and Gerónimo Naranjo was also popular. In addition, there was a demand for traditional New Mexican religious sculpture and secular carvings which were supplied by *santeros* like Celso Gallegos (who sold both wood and stone carvings at the Market), José Dolores Lopez (who carved animals and furniture as well as *santos*), Henry Gonzales (who carved at least one altar besides other pieces), Elias Romero (who carved hat racks as well as religious pieces), Ben Sandoval (who carved *santos* and wooden trays), and the woodcarvers Henry and Robert Brito.

An article in the *Santa Fe New Mexican*, June, 1934, reports that Guadalupe was the most popular *santo* ordered by Native Market customers, but that Santa Barbara had also been requested. Other *santos* made for the Market included Christ on the Cross, St. Michael,

One of the poular wooden burros carved by Leandro Montoya, which was a symbol of the Native Market.

Joseph and the Christ Child, and Saint Rita, and in 1937 Ben Sandoval made a Saint Christopher for a California yacht.

Carved doors were occasionally made by craftsmen. The Market sold numerous smaller items, such as candles made by Jake Brito, willow baskets made by Rose Gonzales of Ilfeld, and wooden buttons made by J.A. Sanchez of Wagon Mound. The most popular items in the Market, which were purchased even on days when nothing else sold, were the little wooden animals, especially the wooden burros with loads of firewood, which were carved by Leandro Montoya.

The Depression years were difficult times in which to start a business. Profit and loss statements show that the Native Market suffered losses each year; consequently Leonora Curtin continued to subsidize it. Nevertheless, the Market's business expanded, and increasing numbers of New Mexican craftsmen profited from the sale of their goods. Total assets for the business went from $4,742.14 (of which $3,330.54 was merchandise inventory) at the end of 1934 to $6,981.87 (of which $5,028.50 was merchandise inventory) at the end of 1935. An article by Wayne Mauzy in *El Palacio,* March-April, 1936, reports that Eleanor Bedell, the Native Market's manager at the time,

> says that the market is now approaching operation on a self-sustaining basis for the first time. This, to the outsider, seems wonderful progress for a period of somewhat less than two years. The rapid increase in furniture sales is largely responsible for this good showing.

In April, 1936 a questionnaire filled out by Eleanor Bedell for a potential New York newspaper article on the Native Market stated that 12 people were employed in the shop. In addition, about 30 weavers, 100 spinners, and 50 furniture makers (or almost 200 craftsmen) contributed to the Market. It is not clear whether this included students at vocational schools, but it probably did not, as there were 32 schools in operation at the time, and many craftsmen were already graduates. A *Christian Science Monitor* article (February, 1937) reported that more than 350 New Mexican village craftsmen earned their living through the Native Market, which nevertheless had difficulty in keeping up with orders.

Additional orders were provided when in the autumn of 1936 a branch store, also called the Native Market, opened in Tucson at the Governor's Corner, where another Santa Fe-based shop, Alice Evans'

Todas Cosas, had already located. The Tucson Native Market, which was managed by Eleanor Bedell and later by Margaret Nelson, sold only crafts made in New Mexico. The Market also developed a successful Santa Fe-based mail order business, with the best markets in the Southwest, California, and New York.

Why was the Native Market so successful? The fact that it was supported financially by Leonora Curtin while it experimented with products and built its reputation was essential to its success. Miss Curtin also provided numerous contacts for the store out of state, acting as a sales representative wherever she went. In addition she offered personal advice and guidance of the most practical kind, seeing the Market as a sort of laboratory for the development of saleable products. Correspondence shows, for example, that when clients complained about the finish on Native Market wooden trays she did research and came up with a prescription for lacquer which worked. She advised spinners to mix a trace of brown hair in heavy white yarn to be used for floor rugs as "a good trick against footprints and soil." She reported at one point that "I have already shown some of the yarn to a possible purchaser whose nose was immediately offended by the odor of goat and I advise segregating the smelly yarn as quickly as possible, keeping it well away from that which has been deodorized." And in 1934 she thought that *colcha* embroidery was a good thing and worth promoting.

The initial success of the Native Market was due not only to the efforts of Miss Curtin but also in large part to the generous support of Santa Fe artists and patrons. As time went on there was increasing business from other areas of the country. The marketability of products was aided by the fact that simplicity was fashionable at the time— Native Market crafts blended well with Bauhaus-style design. Furthermore, Santa Fe had been "discovered"; a 1936 article by Spud Johnson in *Vogue* magazine which joyfully proclaimed Santa Fe to be "a mumble jumble of chumminess" also mentioned the Native Market.

The ultimate success of the Native Market depended upon the development of its role as middleman between two groups that would not normally have met: the urban customer and the rural or small town craftsman. This was reflected in Market advertising, which proclaimed that crafts came "From Village to Market to You." The value of the Native Market to craftsmen is obvious—they could earn money by working at home without disrupting their familiar way of life. At the same time this way of life, and its products, were being admired and elevated by outsiders. Craftsmen in the state proliferated, their work improved, since it had to be of high quality to be purchased, and they were encouraged to produce more goods in less time for higher profit. A typical story of how the Market aided craftsmen was reported in a Washington, D.C. newspaper interview with Leonora Curtin on the Native Market early in 1937. Miss Curtin stated that

> One of the most interesting examples of rehabilitation which has been accomplished through the aid of the shop is that of a wood carver [Ben Sandoval] who has been making images of saints. He sold them to natives and tourists, but would sell perhaps not more than six in a year. His family was hungry and he had no prospect of increasing the revenue his wood carving brought.
> In an effort to adapt his work to public demand, I suggested the making of trays and had him taught to do it. The first trays, over which he spent much time and effort, were quite costly, but contrary to usual custom, as he became more proficient, he charged less for making them and supplied so large a demand, he was able to buy himself a car and a small house in less than a year.

From the customer's point of view, the Native Market offered objects which were not available elsewhere. Romantic advertising played on the idea of New Mexico's remoteness: "Bizarre? [an advertisement queried] No—rather the natural result of an inherent desire in a people of a lovely country to chip pieces from its turquoise sky, its red earth and the eternal green of the mountains and fashion them to daily needs for coolness and warmth, light and shade, comfort and color."

The Market delivered what it advertised. It offered customers quality products at reasonable prices. Typical straight chairs sold for $14.00, rawhide coffeetables for $5.00, pairs of twin beds for $75.00, colcha embroideries for $2.75, and handwoven blankets for $25.00. Also, the Native Market's correspondence shows that every effort was made to be flexible, to satisfy the customer's requests when they were specific, while staying within certain bounds of taste and tradition. Customers often sent initial sketches which became the basis for negotiation. If they were not satisfied with the result, pieces were sometimes re-worked at no additional cost. For example, a typical order calls for "Two panels of screen in Picture No. 9, 4 feet long, 21" wide. To be made like the flowered panel on left in picture, exactly alike, for cupboard doors in a dining room. No legs. Wood edging panel should be wide enough and strong enough to admit small latch and hinges. Color like sample to be sent. Price $15.00."

Besides the success of the Market and the part it played in the rebirth of New Mexico's traditional crafts, the Native Market was good for the city as a whole. All buses of the famous Indian Detours stopped at the Native Market, which was, as Wayne Mauzy said in his *El Palacio* article in 1936, "one of the show places of Santa Fe." For this reason, Miss Curtin was approached with a new idea by several prominent residents of the city in the spring of 1937. They told her that the businessmen of Santa Fe had made a survey of the city to find the main source of its income, and had found through statistical evidence that it was tourism. They added that she was doing the only thing to keep tourists coming to Santa Fe, while "Progress" was destroying the unique charm of the city which attracted tourists. Many people, of course, knew the economic value of tourism to the city—shop, restaurant, and hotel owners and managers of the Indian Detours tour bus company—but not everyone had realized that tourism was the city's major industry. The meeting with Miss Curtin was a preamble to her being asked for the Native Market's cooperation in a tourist venture beyond the scope of anything previously attempted in Santa Fe.

A busy scene at the Native Market. Artist Sheldon Parsons confers with Dolores Perrault (front right), Doña Maria Martinez spins and an unidentified weaver works (left), Pedro Quintana stands in the tinwork booth in front of booth for woven goods (right), and furniture display is in the rear. Note frescoes along the walls. Photo by T. Harmon Parkhurst.

3. El Parian Analco

El Parian Analco ("the meeting place" in the old Indian district of Santa Fe, or "Barrio Analco") was the re-creation of a traditional Spanish New Mexican plaza, with entertainment, restaurants, and various services and booths as well as a shop for sale of crafts. Here visitors to Santa Fe could see something characteristic of the advertised Spanish Southwest, and residents, both Spanish and Anglo, could enjoy an expression of a culture that had been in New Mexico for over three hundred years.

El Parian Analco and the Native Market were established as separate businesses. El Parian was owned by a ten-member Native Market Association, which was led by Leonora Curtin and Major R. Hunter Clarkson, head of the Indian Detour Company and president of the Santa Fe Chamber of Commerce at the time. The Native Market continued as a non-profit corporation, subsidized solely by Miss Curtin. Although the two were legally and financially separate, it was hoped that El Parian would bring customers to the Market, and that Market customers would stroll through El Parian. In addition, it was hoped that the profits made from the entertainment and restaurants at El Parian would help to offset the cost of providing booths for craftsmen at a nominal fee.

El Parian Analco was modeled upon El Parian, which was a thriving market in Santa Fe in the 1880s and 1890s. The old market consisted of numerous booths that ran for about four city blocks along both sides of Galisteo Street from the old Phillips Filling Station (at the Cerrillos Road junction today) to the El Fidel Hotel downtown.

Despite its label, this architect's sketch shows the map of the entire Parian Analco, which includes: a. Native Market, b. La Cocinita, c. El Teatro Analco, d. booths, e. El Restaurante, f. La Cantina, g. El Molino, and h. El Quisco. Photo by Art Taylor.

Livestock, fruit and vegetables, hides and skins, and woven wool goods were hauled in from country villages, and merchandise from Mexico was sold there as well. With Albino Roybal's big dancing hall facing it, El Parian was quite a "meeting place" in its day.

The new El Parian Analco was located across the street from the old San Miguel Mission (rebuilt 1710) and St. Michael's School for boys on College Street (later renamed the Old Santa Fe Trail), three blocks south of the Santa Fe plaza. Two adobe buildings which faced College Street (the Bull Ring restaurant and several shops today) and one and one-half acres of land behind them were leased from the Salazar family. To the south (where the Capitol is today) was the Manderfield house, and to the west was a leafy screen of trees which edged the property of Mrs. Van Stone, curator of the Museum of Fine Arts.

With William Burk, Jr. as architect, Bill Lumpkins as designer, Les Langley as contractor, and thirty workmen, El Parian Analco took shape. The existing buildings housed the Native Market (to the north) and a tortilla mill and restaurant (to the south), with entrance to the enclosed plaza area between them, through massive old wooden gates. Adobe *bancos* (benches) lined the front of the buildings, and the carved wooden burro sign which was the symbol of the Native Market was hung in front of the shop, on College Street.

The plaza was lined with thirty booths for farm produce and crafts. An open air theatre stood in the northwest corner to the rear of the plaza, and a wooden and grillwork bandstand and round outdoor dance floor enclosed by a railing were in the plaza's center. Color was used lavishly on woodwork inside and outside buildings, and scattered fruit trees were planted in the plaza. Parking for fifty cars as well as farm wagons, and corrals for burros, ran along the south wall. Here is how an enthusiastic reporter for the *Santa Fe New Mexican* described El Parian Analco just before its opening:

> The whole layout was made to order, and by breaking through connecting doors in a labyrinth of existing rooms, building additional portales and some small additional adobe houses, the result is ideal for its purposes. . .
>
> In some of the rooms [of the buildings in front] are small square wooden fireplaces, relics of a hundred years ago. The walls in some places are three feet thick; beamed ceilings are blackened with age, nothing is exactly vertical; but the restoration work is making all construction sound and weatherproof. Not a thing is being needlessly changed. . .
>
> No further description is needed than that this enterprise, using old materials, will duplicate a New Mexican native village square of the pregringo period without a note of modernity anywhere in the place; not Spanish, not Mexican, but purely native, colonial New Mexican.

The article also mentions that "The thirty men at work digging into walls and foundations have unearthed most useful old doors and window frames, iron work and so forth and one ancient rude door was completely concealed under plaster and paper."

Following a private pre-opening costume party for 300 the night of August 6, El Parian opened with much pomp on August 7, 1937. Six thousand persons thronged the opening ceremony, which included a blessing by Archbishop Rudolph Aloysius Gerken and a formal address by Governor Clyde Tingley, who declared El Parian officially open, saying "many cities have market places, but none like this. Santa Fe's Native Market is as unique as is the 'Ancient City' itself." Colonel José D. Sena, who acted as master of ceremonies, offered the closing address, in which he explained the purpose of El Parian Analco. He

El Parian Analco under construction. Booths take shape (above), and Leonora Curtin confers with contractor Les Langley (below). Photos by Margaret McKittrick.

announced that El Parian would be open every day and night of the week, and that the daily press and radio would carry news of upcoming sales and entertainment, then concluded by saying the Native Market Association wished it known at the outset that "'El Parian' shall be a happy meeting place for well-behaved citizens . . . Rowdy behavior and drunkenness will not under any circumstances be tolerated, and those who indulge in such practices may expect to be immediately removed from the Market premises."

Within two weeks of its opening, however, El Parian Analco ran into difficulties. The City Council, after hearing objections from St. Michael's School, refused to grant a liquor license to La Cantina, the bar at the rear of El Parian. La Cantina had been open under a license granted by the mayor, but the City Council protested that the decision should have been theirs. The liquor license became a heated issue. The school objected to the close proximity and noise of La Cantina and its potentially bad influence on students. El Parian, represented by Hunter Clarkson, responded that the bar's potential for noise was greatest in the summer when there were no students at the school, that disturbances were minimal, and that profits from La Cantina were necessary to help offset losses sustained from maintaining El Parian. A temporary restraining order was granted by Judge David Chavez, Jr., which allowed La Cantina to sell liquor through the upcoming fiesta, and the issue was eventually resolved in El Parian's favor.

In spite of these initial difficulties, however, El Parian Analco was indeed a meeting place for Santa Feans. Besides La Cantina, El Restaurante del Parian offered traditional New Mexican meals, and La Cocinita served lighter meals under the portal near the bandstand. A *Santa Fe New Mexican* article (June 4, 1938) reports that

'Pollo Borracho' was conceived as a new Spanish dish at the Cocinita of El Parian last night as members of the cast and audience jammed the tiny kitchen following the Santa Fe Little Theatre production at Teatro Analco. The chicken steeped in wine and covered with pinones, is dedicated to 'The Drunkard' with its title of 'drunken chicken.'

In addition to the bar and restaurants, food was provided at El Parian Analco by a tortilla mill and booths of home-grown New Mexico produce, in season. El Molino, the authentic leather and wood tortilla mill, ground corn, turned meal to dough, and produced tortillas and *chicharrones* (cracklings), and sold tacos, tamales, enchiladas, tostadas,

La Cocinita, its menu painted on the wall. Photo by Margaret McKittrick.

and chile (red always, green in season). A *Santa Fe New Mexican* announcement of El Parian Analco's specials in produce for the week includes a dozen ears of corn, 19¢; a pound of cooking apples, 3¢; large cucumbers, 1¢; a pound of Flemish pears, 6¢; a pound of large pod green chiles, 6¢; a pound of white onions, 4¢; a pound of apricots, 3¢; and two large bunches of carrots, 5¢. Other booths offered services like horseshoeing and knife sharpening, and sold such items as Spanish baked goods and Mexican candy, and *leña* (firewood) could be ordered from El Parian to be delivered to the home by burro.

There were also booths for the sale of Spanish New Mexican arts and crafts. The *Santa Fe Plaza* (August 7, 1937) lists the following crafts in booths: E.D. Trujillo (Chimayo blankets), Emilio Padilla (wood carving), José R. Ortega (tie weaving), Frank Garcia (tin working), Manuel Montoya (knife carving), Ben Sandoval (wooden trays), Velarde Blind Children (brushes), and Church Booth (tallow candles). The crafts booths did not last long, however; as Leonora Paloheimo later commented, "The booths proved the significant fact that in an American economy, workers cannot afford the time to sit." After the booths were abandoned some of these craftsmen continued to produce crafts

Produce day at El Parian with a wagon from Rio en Medio in the foreground. Note the "Ride the Burro" sign in the rear. Photo by Margaret McKittrick.

objects, which they sold or left on consignment at the Native Market.

Native New Mexican singing and music for dancing were offered by a talented pianist and local groups like Los Villeros Alegres and La Tipica Zacateña, as well as by visiting musicians, with a general admission charge of 10¢ for the evening, and dancing at 10¢ per dance or 76¢ for the evening. One of the most popular attractions at El Parian was the folk dancing to which each Wednesday night was devoted. (Modern dancing was allowed on other nights, but New Mexican folk dancing seems to have dominated on those nights as well.) The El Parian Folk Lore group (consisting of eight couples) executed traditional New Mexican folk dances which were then taught to the general public by the *bastonero* (dance master), Vicente Gallegos. Mrs. Paloheimo recalls that "After the tourists went home, what was the management's consternation to receive letters of request from orchestras in various cities over the country asking for music of these New Mexico folk dances! Their customers, they said, insisted upon it."

The *Santa Fe New Mexican* joyfully proclaimed (August 18, 1938) that

> Everyone's Dancing La Raspa as Fiesta Season Approaches . . .
> Santa Fe dancers continue to surprise tourists with their addiction to folk dancing which is shown not only during summer months, building to a Fiesta climax, but throughout the entire year at formal and informal parties. When the Native Market this summer began its Wednesday night program devoted to folk dancing,

even the sponsors little dreamed of the enthusiastic response to follow. Last night there were nearly 400 persons at El Parian to participate in the dances on the attractive little open-air platform [El Quisco] until the rain came, then to move into all the lovely old rooms surrounding el restaurante and into the restaurant itself, to continue the dancing.

The article goes on to describe the dances, which included La Raspa ("danced to a polka tempo with swinging foot movements on a broken rhythm"—scraping leather soles caused the rasping sound), La Camilla (a waltz "in which the unexpected music stops bring excitment and laughter to the dancers"), La Chinche (the Rye Waltz, but danced as though "the couple were trying to step on a bug, and upon doing so, they waltzed around"), and waltzes like La Indita (The Little Indian) and El Vaquero (The Cowboy), as well as the Schottische, the "ever present Varsoviana, and the inevitable Cuadrillas."

A guidebook to the dances which appeared in 1937, *Folk-Dances of the Spanish-Colonials of New Mexico* by Helene Mareau, Eunice Hauskins, and Aurora Lucero-White, stated that the colonial New Mexican dances were folk descendants of continental European dances which were introduced into Mexico by Polish émigrés following the Polish Revolution, and later reinforced during the brief empire of Maximilian and Carlotta. The Polish dances, which, like other things Mexican, travelled north to New Mexico, were later banned in Mexico, but New Mexico retained and modified them.

Performers stroll through El Parian's gate.

Another popular feature at El Parian was Los Aficionados, or amateur night, which was held on several Saturday nights in August, 1937, with crowds of 1500-2500 recorded in attendance. In the summer of 1938 Los Aficionados was replaced by a series of Corridas de Canciones, group singing of traditional New Mexico songs, each Sunday evening. The intent was to revive the spirit of Santa Fe just a few years earlier, when (as the *Santa Fe New Mexican* reminisced June 9, 1938), "the city plaza and every hall in town resounded with music." The article goes on to say that "Alex Flores, the genial, pink-shirted violinist" and his six-piece orchestra will accompany Juanito Valdez and his chorus, and featured singer Concha Ortiz y Pino, in leading familiar Spanish folk tunes. Words of the songs were flashed on a screen so that all present could participate. Las Corridas were immensely popular, with 700 participants the first evening and even larger crowds in the following weeks. They included contests for dancers, singers, and instrumentalists, with a $5.00 prize to the first place winner for the evening. The *Santa Fe New Mexican*, June 9, 1938, announced that contestants for the next Corridas would include five-year-old Pauline Lucero as well as four adult singers, three dance teams, and a solo dancer, and Jake Berry, a ten-year-old marimba artist from St. Michael's School. According to the *Santa Fe New Mexican*, June 13, 1938, the winners of this contest were Miss Dolores White, with a recitation and a song (first place); Miss Consuelo Lucero and Celso Lopez, who danced in "stunning black satin costumes" (second place); and the five-year-old singer Pauline Lucero (third place).

Although the outdoor season closed at the end of September, dancing continued through October and November of 1937 and 1938. The *Santa Fe New Mexican*, Oct. 23, 1937, reported that "The dancing at El Parian these evenings is getting better and better . . . . a lot of the gang seems to like food mixed with music and exercise," and (Nov. 27, 1937) that "An excellent remedy for that stuffed and dopey feeling is a little dancing with your meals." When even the most intrepid dancers retired for the 1937 and 1938 seasons the plaza at El Parian was flooded for ice skating, and on December 22, 1937, 1,200 children consumed 650 quarts of milk, 350 dozen doughnuts, 900 pounds of candy, and 34 boxes of apples at El Parian's Christmas party.

A focal point of festivities at El Parian was its open air theatre—El Teatro Analco—which was located in the northwest corner at the rear of the plaza. The 1937 season was highlighted by the St. Francis Players'

The plaza at El Parian Analco: A view toward El Restaurante and the gate shows the facade of St. Michael's School in the background (above); visitors stroll past El Quisco, the dance floor (below). Photos by Margaret McKittrick.

production of "The Sheep of San Cristobal," a miracle play of New Mexico folklore which was adapted by local writer Raymond Otis from the story by Frank Applegate. In the summer of 1938 the Santa Fe Little Theatre performed a series of plays at El Teatro Analco. As a member of the group, Dana Jones, recalled years later,

> We opened to wild enthusiasm with "The Drunkard," . . .
>
> That was the beginning of the long, happy summer. I will never forget it. We practically lived at the Market, building sets, rehearsing, performing at night. The Native Market was a world of its own; a city within a city.

Dana Jones' recollections continue in what is called the "Life Was Simpler Dept.":

> One day three of us decided that we needed one of the Plaza benches for our current set. They were not fastened down, but they were not easily portable, so we were struggling. A member of the local Police Force materialized and asked us what we were doing. We told him. He called to a few interested bystanders and together we managed to drag the thing up College Street and onto the stage.

Mel Marshall as the villain in "The Drunkard" at El Teatro Analco. Candles behind sconces light the stage.

Besides "The Drunkard" the 1938 season at Teatro Analco included "One Mad Night," "A Ready Made Family," "Three-Cornered Moon," "Murder in the Red Barn," and "Nelly the Bandit's Sweetheart, or It Can't Happen in Burro Alley." The *Santa Fe New Mexican*, Aug. 27, 1938, reports that "Nelly," which was the 1938 Fiesta melodrama, was adapted by Raymond Otis from an old dime novel about Billy the Kid by "an Englishman who had never seen Billy nor the Southwest, but who had heard about both. Blood-curdles are never sacrificed to accuracy in either novel or play." The Santa Fe Little Theatre went on to purchase its own building and make its mark on theatre in Santa Fe, but "no group," Dana Jones recalls, "ever had such a happy beginning."

El Parian Analco was the setting for many happy events—parties were held there, and tourists were taken there without fail. Mrs. Paloheimo recalls overhearing enthusiastic tourists from Chicago exclaim that "There is nothing like this in Mexico!" El Parian was a center for fiesta activities. A letter from El Parian to the Fiesta Council (Aug. 5, 1938) offers the following events as its contribution to that year's fiesta: El Parian Spanish Orchestra, El Parian Folk Dance Group, El Parian Spanish Quartette, El Parian Spanish Variety Show, a bullfight in El Parian Plaza (!), open air dancing, barbeque, community singing of Spanish songs, and a roof show at La Fonda. Dana Jones recalls that the 1938 Fiesta Comedy Parade was graced by Ray Eubank, El Teatro Analco's entry, who, in a thespian mood, wore a white sheet and vine leaves and manned a small chariot pulled by a motorcycle.

In the midst of all this gaiety, the Native Market continued the serious work of marketing traditional New Mexican crafts. The Market's new quarters ran back from the street along the north side of the plaza through a series of rooms like train cars, a showroom in front followed by an office, storage and wool dyeing area, carpentry room, and painting, decorating, and finishing shops. The soft adobe walls, low ceilings, and uneven wood floors of the old building provided a homey environment for the workers and their crafts, and adventures for wandering tourists.

The staff was headed by Janette Lumpkins, who managed the Native Market at El Parian from the autumn of 1937 through the end of 1939. (She replaced Margaret Nelson, who moved to Tucson in 1937 to manage the Native Market there.) Mrs. Lumpkins, a painter, had originally been hired as a color consultant when the new Native Market was being designed. When she could spare the time from her work as

A Native Market rug is apparently being washed and rinsed. El Quisco is to the rear.

manager, which included the coordination of production with sales and shipment, displays, ordering and issuing of raw materials, and bookkeeping, she helped with furniture decoration in the Market's finishing shop.

The *Santa Fe Plaza*, Aug. 1, 1937, listed the craftsmen at El Parian as:

Weavers—E.D. Trujillo, José Ramon Ortega of Chimayo, the latter in charge of weaving neckties; Alfredo Catanach, Valentin Rivera, Max Ortiz.
Spinners—Donaciana Romero, Lena Barela.
Finishers, Refugio Leyba.
Embroidery, Deolinda Baca.
Tinwork, Eddy Delgado, Pedro Quintana.
Woodworkers; Ben Sandoval, Abad Lucero, Ben Lujan, Ramon Martinez, two boys from Taos.

Some of these craftsmen (as well as many others not on this list, such as Eloy Chavez, the furniture maker) worked in their own shops or homes, taking orders from the Market or selling completed pieces there. The regular staff at the Native Market, in addition to Janette Lumpkins, included most of the craftsmen who had worked at the Palace Avenue Native Market: Tillie Gabaldon, dyeing and *colcha* embroidery; Deolinda Baca, *colcha* embroidery and weaving; Valentin Rivera and Filiberto Salazar, weaving; Refugio Leyba and David Lammlae, fur-

Valentin Rivera at work on a narrow white mohair rug (above), and a wider piece (below) at the Native Market.

niture finishing and painting (Lammlae also painted glass and tin); Eliseo Rodriguez, painting and leaded glass; Ben Sandoval, woodworking; and Pedro Quintana, tinsmithing.

Abad Lucero, who had made furniture in his Santa Fe shop for the Native Market on Palace Avenue, had gone on to teach in the vocational schools at Taos and Mora, then opened a furniture making shop with Elidio Gonzales, one of his students, in Taos. Lucero returned to Santa Fe in 1938 to manage the El Parian Native Market's furniture production. Working in his own shop in Santa Fe, Lucero was given orders for furniture from the Native Market, which he filled with the assistance of two craftsmen from Mora, then sent in to the Market for shipping. It is interesting to note that Lucero had originally developed an interest in furniture making through looking at old pieces owned by his uncle in Peña Blanca. He took manual training in high school, then began to make furniture in Santa Fe in 1929, basing his designs on old pieces that he saw in The Spanish Chest, an antique shop in Santa Fe owned by Benny Sweringen.

Textiles, furniture, and tinwork were the mainstays at the El Parian Native Market, as they had been in the Palace Avenue store. While purchases in the shop were greatest in the summer months, Native Market business was less seasonal than that of El Parian as a whole, and winter sales were boosted by the Tucson shop. As the Native Market's reputation grew increasing business came through mail orders (by way of the Tucson shop as well as the one in Santa Fe). The Market secured several prestigious large jobs for the furnishing of hotels, including the Santa Fe Inn, a quiet hotel/retreat (a monastery today), for which the market made furniture, *colcha* embroidered drapery and bedspreads, tinwork fixtures, and rugs; the Hotel Paso del Norte in El Paso, for which furniture and tinwork were made; and the Albuquerque Hilton, for which the Market and numerous vocational schools made furniture and other fixtures. Ceramic ashtrays made by the Native Market for the Hilton were stamped with a device which read "This ashtray taken from the Albuquerque Hilton," in anticipation of their popularity.

Correspondence and order forms show that between 1937 and 1939 the Native Market did considerable business with craftsmen at the Taos Vocational School and with Elias Romero, who was a furniture maker in Las Vegas. The Market also continued to work with craftsmen from small villages, such as Elviria Tapia and Mrs. Fidel Baca (spinning,

Typical sketches, based on customers' orders, from which Native Market craftsmen worked. Photos by Art Taylor.

FIRE - SCREEN

FRAME - ¾" I ROD

DECORATION AT TOP ¾" STRAP IRON

BOTTOM - 28"
HEIGHT - 37"

NOTE!
PLEASE SEND A TRACING ON
WRAPPING PAPER OF EXACT
SIZE OF OPENING OF FIREPLACE
SO THAT CURVE AND
SIZE OF FRAME MAY BE
DETERMINED

NATIVE MARKET
SANTA FE

Atrisco), Ben Lovato (goatskins, Hernandez), Antonia Cruz (spinning, Chimayo), Aurelia Candelaria (*colcha* embroidery, Puerto de Luna), and Ramon Martinez (furniture making, Mora).

Local interest in New Mexico's Spanish colonial crafts was reflected in an attempt to reactivate the Spanish Colonial Arts Society in February, 1938. A meeting of forty members, former members, and interested friends of the society met at Leonora Curtin's home to discuss various projects that might be undertaken. Although the Society remained essentially inactive until 1952, it did sponsor a large exhibit of Spanish colonial arts and crafts in the Fine Arts Museum which opened in August, 1938. Miss Curtin conceived the idea of the exhibit because it seemed to her that as most of the old crafts pieces had been bought by dealers and private collectors, many New Mexicans had no idea what colonial New Mexican crafts were like. She proceded to borrow furniture, textiles, carvings, and tinwork from New Mexico friends for the show. When she was asked to reproduce the exhibit for the New Mexico entry at the New York World's Fair of 1939-40, she declined out of respect for the safety of treasures in the possession of people who loved them—and the state went unrepresented.

Meanwhile, the problems of time-consuming, custom-made crafts (with their attendant difficulties in coordination and negotiation) were an ongoing concern at the Market. Leonora Curtin wrote to Janette Lumpkins in April, 1938 that

> It worries me that time should be such a problem for you, and furthermore, if we don't succeed in getting some things to take care of themselves without your constant personal attention, we'll never make the Market earn money in just proportion. But how to make a good quantity of marketable stock materialize without this attention, is the everlasting problem. Standardization? Yes, but how and what? Well, there are certain types of things—and the time will come. Meanwhile, we are apt to lose track of the problem and the aim in the stress of filling special orders; yet without the special orders, what? A wholesale business? Yes, but then there is the difficulty of getting the prices low enough, etc . . .

Native Market profit and loss statements from 1938 show that it continued to suffer financial losses in its new location. The business was still expanding, but Miss Curtin still subsidized it.

Although the Native Market continued to operate, El Parian Analco was forced to close after the 1938 summer season. Only the restaurant stayed open, under the management of Luis Salazar and ownership of the Salazar family. Almost all of the original shareholders of El Parian had dropped out, and the idealistic venture had proven to be on too large a scale to support itself.

In addition, a severe fire in the fall of 1938 destroyed most of the west side of the plaza, leaving even the theatre in ashes. El Parian Analco was used one more time. The *Santa Fe New Mexican* announced (July 29, 1939) that "The Native Market which has been closed so far this year will be open for the Fiesta . . .A part of the Market is being reconstructed and remodeled so that a restaurant-bar and dance pavilion will be open for the use of Fiesta revelers." The Market itself had remained open, so this presumably is meant to refer to El Parian Analco as a whole. True to its name, El Parian Analco had been a meeting place, affording rich opportunities for the friendly mingling of people, and its closing was a sad event for residents and visitors alike.

Then, at the end of 1939, a crafts guild, the Alianza de Artesanos (otherwise known as the Native Market Guild) was formed and took over the ownership and management of the Native Market from Miss Curtin. As she later reminisced,

> . . . the nation and the world showed unmistakable signs of recovery from the low years of depression, and when the numbers of skilled craftsmen had multiplied throughout the state, largely owing to the training received in a total of 32 Vocational Schools, it was time for the Native Market to stand on its own feet . . . . it was this organization of craftsmen, the Alianza de Artesanos, which duly assumed the operation and the functions of the Native Market—an endeavor which had from the outset, been theirs in a real sense.

The Alianza was a cooperative selling guild composed of twenty-three craftsmen as charter members, with a committee of non-members to judge potential new members on the basis of their skills and the authenticity of their work in the New Mexican Spanish tradition. The committee consisted of three authorities on Spanish colonial crafts: Truman Mathews, an architect; Kenneth Chapman, an anthropologist with the Laboratory of Anthropology; and Brice Sewell, who was still State Director of Vocational Trade and Industrial Education. Leslie Cornish, a woodworker who had taught at the Taos Vocational School, was in charge of the Market, and Lolita Harper was in charge of sales. Advertisements for the Alianza show that the same sort of crafts were sold as had been previously offered at the Native Market. Merchandise that remained when the Alianza took over the Market was left on consignment by Leonora Curtin. New crafts objects were taken on consignment by the Market from the craftsmen.

The Alianza Native Market only stayed open for about six months, however. Survival was difficult without Miss Curtin's support. Also, federal programs like the WPA and NYA (National Youth Administration) attracted some craftsmen, more high paying jobs became available, and then with the Nation's entrance into World War II the New Mexico crafts revival came to a halt, as the demand for skilled work drew almost every available craftsman into critical employment. Many New Mexico craftsmen were sent to California to work as shipwrights, having learned to read blueprints and build from them in New Mexico's vocational schools. Bill Lumpkins recalls seeing a busload of woodworkers and other craftsmen pull away from the Santa Fe plaza—a sign on the side of their bus read "New Mexico Workers for the War Effort." Little did the public realize what a triumph this sign represented.

When Brice Sewell joined the Navy in 1943 his assistant, Henry Gonzales, took over as Director of Vocational Trade and Industrial Education, a position which he held into the early 1950s. After Gonzales' retirement the vocational program switched its emphasis again to trades such as welding. Times had changed—Los Alamos had come into existence, Albuquerque had become a large city—and most young people were interested in learning more lucrative trades than traditional craftsmanship. Some of the older craftsmen continued to work in their crafts after World War II, however, and still serve as links between past and present today; for example, Elidio Gonzales still has a furniture shop in Taos, Abad Lucero still makes furniture in Albuquerque, Tillie Gabaldon Stark does *colcha* embroidery in Santa Fe, and in Rivera, west of Santa Fe, David Salazar is weaving again after retirement from the railroad.

Following the waning popularity of post war "modern" styles, crafts became popular once more in the 1960s and 1970s. Young Spanish New Mexican craftsmen are again learning traditional styles and techniques, and many of the Anglo-made crafts in New Mexico, notably furniture and vegetable-dyed woven goods, also show the influence of traditional Spanish New Mexican crafts. The Spanish Colonial Arts Society, which was reactivated in 1952, once again sponsors the Spanish Market on the Santa Fe plaza the last weekend in July each year. And the Colonial New Mexico Historical Foundation has

Joe Mendoza (left, with wooden pitchfork) and others look on as bread is removed from the horno, or outdoor oven at a festival at El Rancho de las Golondrinas. Photo by Y.A. Paloheimo.

Traditional maternal and paternal grandparents' houses, built next to the main house at the Mountain Village, Rancho de las Golondrinas. Photo by Y.A. Paloheimo.

re-created a living museum south of Santa Fe where traditional Spanish colonial ranch activities, and singing and dancing, may be viewed at a series of open houses from spring through autumn each year. An integral part of the spring and fall festivals at the Rancho de las Golondrinas are the booths where craftsmen sell traditional Spanish New Mexican crafts. A new Cultural Center at the Ranch will provide space for several groups concerned with the state's Spanish heritage, including Los Caballeros DeVargas, La Sociedad Folklorica, and a newly formed guild for Spanish New Mexican craftsmen, tentatively named La Cofradía de Artes y Artesanos Hispanico. A permanent exhibition of the guild's finest crafts will be housed in their Guild Hall, filling one floor of the Cultural Center. These buildings, activities, and crafts, like those of the Native Market and the state's vocational program in the 1930s, are a testimonial to the fact that the culture of Spanish New Mexico was and still is unique, not to be confused with the Indian or Anglo cultures in the state, or with the culture of Old Mexico.

As we stand on the threshhold of a new revival of Spanish New Mexican crafts, we should be thankful for the crafts movement of the 1930s, which came at a crucial time. Because of the united efforts of craftsmen, educators, and patrons, each of whom gave something vital to the others, the Spanish New Mexican crafts tradition was revived and many New Mexicans were helped to survive during those difficult years. Designs and techniques of craftsmanship were close enough to those employed in earlier models that the crafts of the 1930s can be considered part of the same tradition. Their adaptations to modern life and expressions of individual creativity mark them as part of a living tradition rather than simply copies. Today Native Market crafts are considered collectibles, and are widely sought after. Many pieces of Native Market furniture, woven goods, and other crafts objects can be found in New Mexico homes, as sturdy and handsome as ever.

Furniture

Chest with relief carved rosettes on stand, painted brown and rubbed for antique effect.
Photo by Art Taylor.

Dark green painted chest and stand decorated with leaves and flowers, birds, and uniformed figures in boats. Iron lock, hasp, and hinges are Native Market made. Photo by Art Taylor.

Chest on stand, painted black with white and yellow rosettes and white, blue, yellow, and red leaves. Native Market ironwork hasp and lock. Photo by Y.A. Paloheimo.

Chest with legs, with three top and eight front panels. Traditional painted flower and animal decorations on each panel.

Chest of drawers—a modern piece, but with traditional rosettes, their centers acting as drawer pulls.

Trastero with one door, hand carved spindles, single drawer, shell crest. Painted yellow, with red and green flower and leaf decorations. Photo by Art Taylor.

Trastero with same basic structure as piece on previous page, but with natural finish, more elaborately carved spindles, shell drawer pulls, and scallops on sides of shell crest. Photo by Art Taylor.

The trastero with double doors, elaborately carved spindles, grooved lower door panels and shell crest is attributed to Tomás C de Baca. (Priest's chair, tin painted lamp with painted shade, chair, table, striped rug and wood carving are all Native Market products.)

Table and matching bench with carved uprights. (Also, Native Market made set of chairs, repisa, and chest.)

Table with carved legs, additional leaves which swing out to rest on supports, with matching bench, both attributed to Tomás C de Baca.

Desk with side and middle drawers, carved with rosettes. This is a modern piece which uses traditional proportions and decorative motif. (Chairs with and without arms, rug, carved burro, tin mirror and vase, and wood and tin lantern—see drawing p. 50—are all Native Market made.)

Writing desk on stand, with relief carved lions, rosettes, and pomegranates, modelled on old chests but opening in front to reveal compartments within.

Writing desk on cabinet base with relief carved lions, scallops, and rosettes and overlaid diamonds. Dark natural finish. Photo by Art Taylor.

Table-chair with drawer. Top swings up for chair, down for table. This is not a traditional New Mexico piece, but proportions are typical for a New Mexico priest's chair. Photo by Art Taylor.

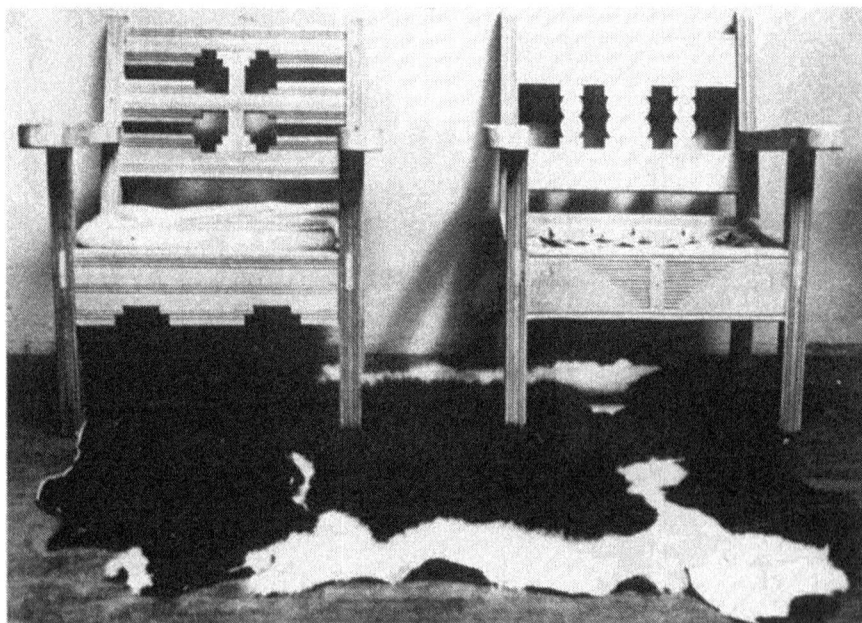

Carved priest's chairs (chairs with arms) with woven leather seats, one with added pillow.

Four typical Native Market side chairs. (Note colcha embroidered upholstered seat on chair, upper left.)

Priest's chair and side chair, both with woven rawhide seats and carved grooves, priest's chair with shell crest. Photo by Art Taylor.

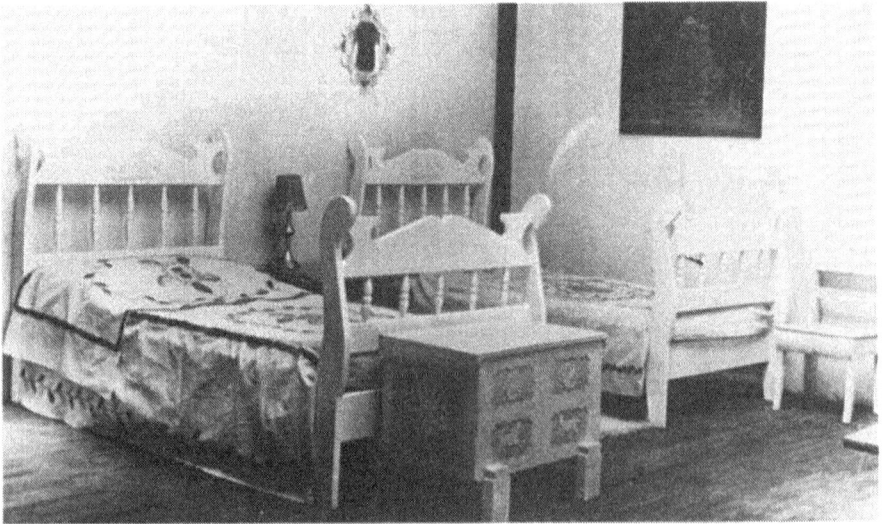

Empire style matching twin beds, painted white, with painted headboard decorations. (Native Market made colcha bedspreads and carved chest.)

Empire style single bed with relief-carved rosette on headboard, teardrop shaped cutouts on footboard. (Small bedside table, dresser modelled upon chest but opening outward, painted chest under window, santo, tin mirror, candelabras, box, and lamp, and colcha bedspread, all Native Market made.)

Couch with sloping arms, scalloped back, spindles across front. (Native Market tables, lamps, and rug.)

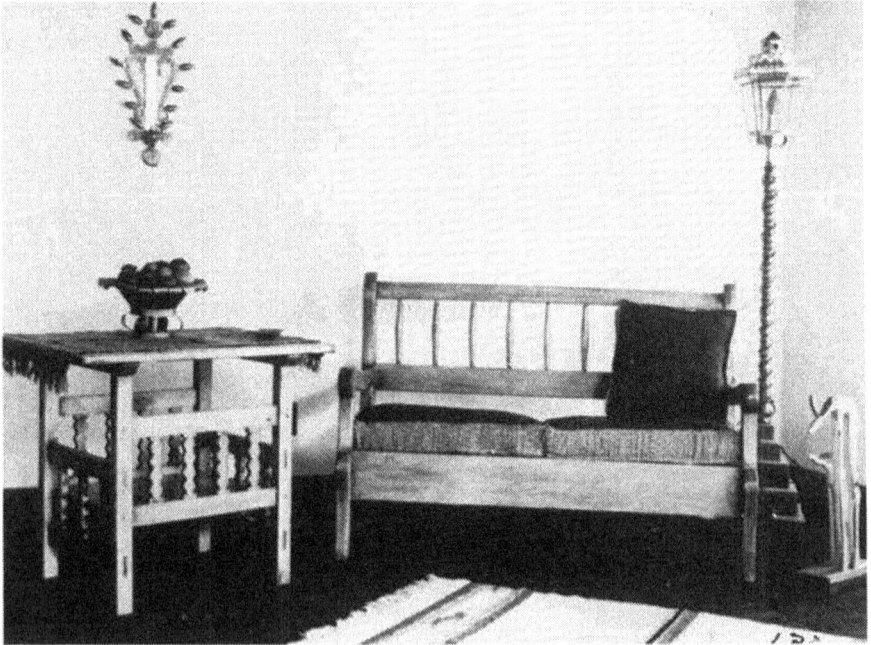

Small couch with spindles across back. (Native Market tin fruit bowl, Celso Gallegos carving, torch.)

"Taos bed" style couch, with uniform height back and arms, hand carved spindles. (Native Market rugs and colcha pillows.)

Chupadero chair and table, hand sewn. (Tinwork and pillows are Native Market made.)

Hand carved door with overlaid geometric designs, exposed nail heads.

Textiles

Weft faced plain weave rug in vegetable-dyed colors of dark brown, brown, beige, gold, rose, orange, and blue-green. Photo by Art Taylor.

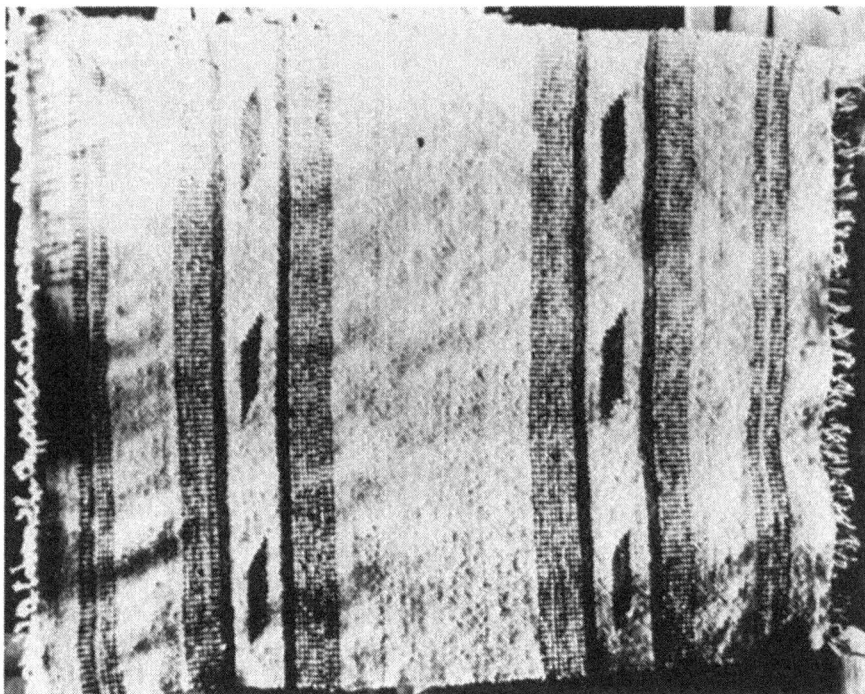

Plain weave rug with tapestry weave designs.

Plain weave rug with traditional tapestry weave chevron and hourglass designs.

Plaid twill weave blanket in vegetable-dyed colors of brown, rust, blue, and white. Photo by Art Taylor.

Black and white twill rug with herringbone and diamond weaves. Photo by Art Taylor.

Black and white twill rug with diamond weave. Photo by Art Taylor.

Small blankets of plain weave (left), float weave (top), and twill (bottom, middle, and right).

Multi-colored colcha embroidered pillows employing zigzag, flower, and bird motifs.

Multi-colored colcha embroidered pillows with traditional zigzag, flower, and animal motifs. (Pillow in upper right woven at the Native Market.) Photo by Art Taylor.

Tinwork

Stamped tin chandelier in plant design, for 8 candles. Photo by Art Taylor.

Tin hanging lantern with stamped rosette design.

Elaborately stamped tin cross and mirror.

82

Stamped tin lamp and mirrors with lights.

A variety of stamped tin candleholders.

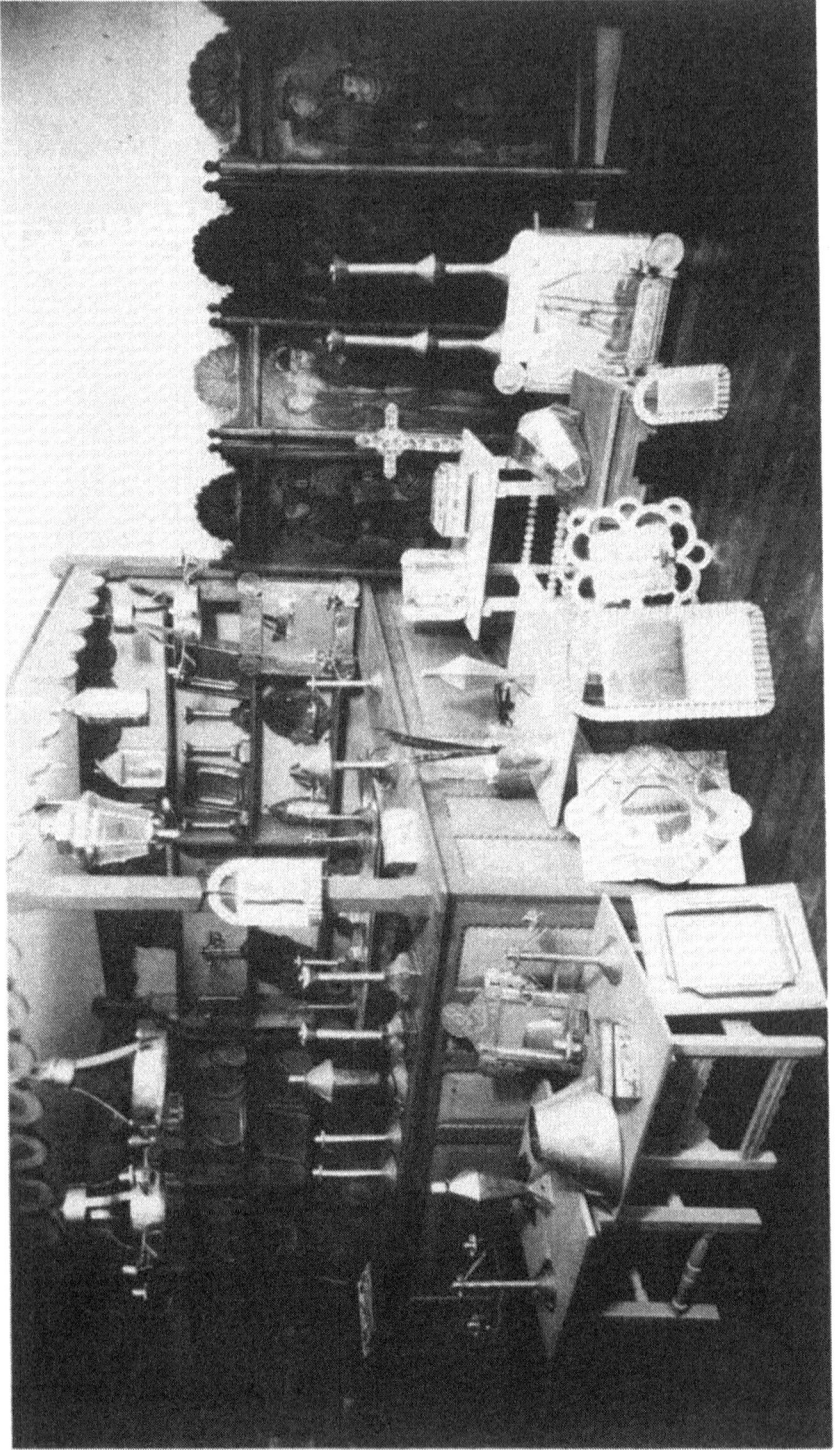

Tin on display at the Palace Avenue Native Market, showing the variety of tin objects sold.

Woodwork

Wooden trays were not used in colonial New Mexico, but the traditional design motifs of scallops and crowned lions flanking a pomegranate have been used in this Native Market piece.

Carved animals by Leandro Montoya. Oxen and plowman (top), ox and covered wagon (bottom).

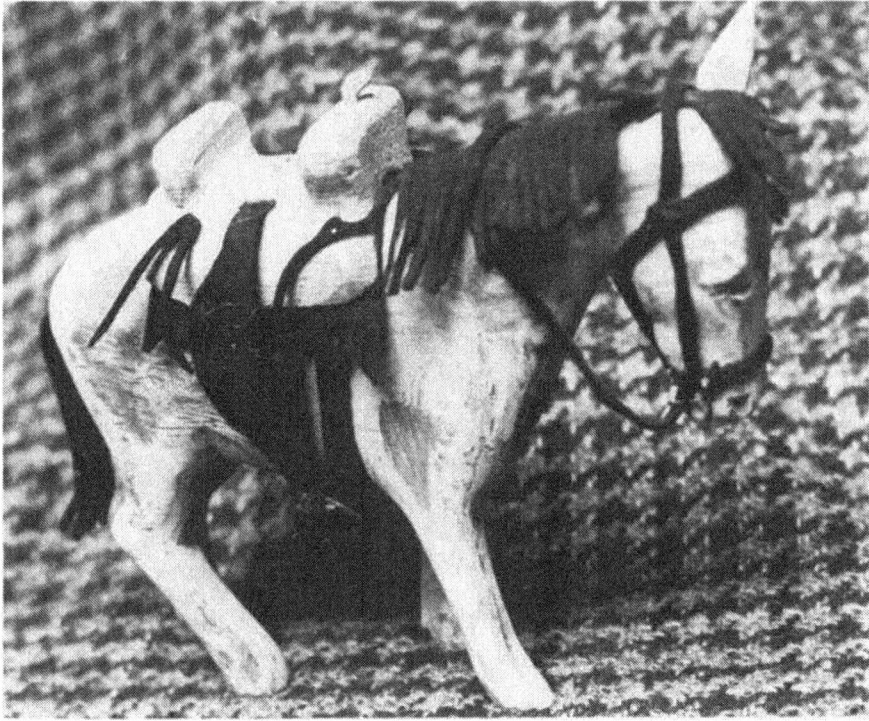

Carved animals by Leandro Montoya. Horse with saddle and bridle (top), and deer drinking from mirror pond (bottom).

Retablo by Fred Sandoval. Subject is unclear, bearing some resemblance to a bishop but with a multiple-tiered hat. Photo by Y.A. Paloheimo.

Display of Native Market woodwork, including chair, chest, stool, trays, carved animals (by Leandro Montoya, top shelf, and unknown artist, bottom right) and santos, including Guadalupe and Christ on the Cross.

Photo Credits

All Native Market Collection photos were taken in the 1930s, unless otherwise indicated.

NMC: Native Market Collection
NNM: Museum of New Mexico

Page
4 MNM
5 MNM
7 Spanish Colonial Arts Society, Inc., in the collections of the MNM
   NMC, 1978
9 NMC
10 NMC
13 NM Education Department
15 NMC
   NMC
16 NMC
   NMC
19 NMC
   NMC
20 NMC
21 NMC
22 NMC
24 NMC
   NMC
26 NMC
27 NMC, 1978
28 MNM
29 NMC
30 NMC
34 NMC
36 William E. Burk, Jr., Architect
38 NMC
   NMC
40 NMC
41 NMC
42 NMC
44 NMC
   NMC
45 NMC
47 NMC

48 NMC
   NMC
50 NMC, 1978
   NMC, 1978
54 Y.A. Paloheimo, 1976
   Y.A. Paloheimo, 1976
57 NMC, 1978
58 NMC, 1978
   Y.A. Paloheimo, 1978
59 NMC
   NMC
60 NMC, 1978
61 NMC, 1978
62 NMC
   NMC
63 NMC
   NMC
64 NMC
65 NMC, 1978
66 NMC, 1978
   NMC
67 NMC
   NMC
   NMC
   NMC
68 NMC, 1978
   NMC
69 NMC
70 NMC
   NMC
71 NMC
72 NMC
73 NMC
74 NMC, 1978
75 NMC
   NMC
76 NMC, 1978
77 NMC, 1978
78 NMC, 1978
79 NMC

80 NMC
  NMC, 1978
81 NMC, 1978
82 NMC
  NMC
83 NMC
  NMC
84 NMC

85 NMC
86 NMC
  NMC
87 NMC
  NMC
88 Y.A. Paloheimo, 1978
89 NMC

Line drawings on pages v, vii, 1, 11, 35, 55 and 97 are taken from a brochure for the Native Market Guild printed in 1940, now in the Native Market Collection.

Index

*denotes illustration

Roybal, Albino, 36
Saint Francis Players, 43
Saint Michael's School, 36, 39
Salazar, David, 21, 25, 26*, 53
Salazar family, 36
Salazar, Filiberto, 47
Salazar, Luis, 36, 51-52
Sanchez, J.A., 31
Sandoval, Ben, 30, 31, 33, 40, 47, 49
Sandoval, Francisco, 29
Sandoval, Fred, 88*
San Miguel Mission, 36
Santa Fe Fiesta, 46
Santa Fe Inn, 49
Santa Fe Little Theatre, 45, 46
Santa Fe Trail, 2
Santeros and *santos*, 2, 3, 5-6, 20,
    30-31, 69*, 88*, 89*. *See also*
    Gallegos, Celso and Lopez, José
    Dolores
Schoen, Roy, 21
Sena, Col. José D., 37
Sewell, Brice, 10, 12, 13, 14, 17, 18,
    29, 52, 53
"Sheep of San Cristobal," 45
Singing, 6, 42*, 43, 55
Sketches, working, 13, 50*
Smith-Hughes Act, 12
Southwest Arts and Crafts shop, 4
Spanish and Indian Trading Com-
    pany, 5, 23
Spanish Arts shop, 8-9, 9*
Spanish Chest, The, 49
Spanish Colonial Arts Society, Inc.,
    6, 8, 9, 11, 51, 53
Spanish colonists, 1-2
Spanish Market, 8, 53
Spinning, carding and, 6, 10*, 18,
    19*, 20, 21, 22*, 23, 24*, 25,
    31, 34*, 47, 49, 51
Stools, 28
Stores, 3-5, 8-9, 23, 31, 32, 49.
    See also Native Market, El Parian
    and Native Market, Palace Avenue
Style, New Mexican Spanish crafts,
    1, 2, 3, 13-14, 25, 26, 27-29,

55, 57-89*
Sweringen, Benny, 49
Tables, 20, 28, 29, 33, 62*, 63*,
    69*, 70*
Tafoya, Manuel, 25
Taos beds (couches), 14, 28, 70*, 71*
Tapia, Elviria, 49
"Three-Cornered Moon," 46
Tingley, Governor Clyde, 37
Tinwork, 3, 9, 13, 17, 18, 20, 21,
    23, 28*, 29-30, 29*, 34*, 40, 47,
    48, 49, 62*, 63, 69*, 70*, 72*,
    81-84*
Todas Cosas, 32
Trade, Mexican, 2
Trasteros, 14, 20, 27, 60*, 61*, 62*
Trujillo, E.D., 40, 47
Trujillo, Pilar, 23
Valdez, Juanito, 43
Van Stone, Mrs., 36
Varguenos. See Desks
Velarde blind children, 40
Vigil, Agnes, 23
Vigil, Pablo, 30
Villiaseñor, David, 21
Vocational schools, 10*, 12-18, 13*,
    18, 19*, 52; Abiquiu, 17; Agua
    Fria, 17; Anton Chico, 17, 23;
    Atarque, 17; Bernalillo, 17; Chu-
    padero, 14, 15*, 17, 23; Cienega,
    17; Costilla, 17; Cundiyo, 17; Es-
    pañola, 17; Galisteo, 17, 25;
    Grants, 17; Las Vegas, 17; Limitar,
    17; Los Lunas, 17; Mora, 17, 23,
    49; Peñasco, 17; Portales, 17;
    Puerto de Luna, 17; Rio en Medio,
    16*, 23; Roswell, 17; San José,
    17, 25; Santa Cruz, 17; Socorro,
    17; Taos, 14, 17, 18, 49, 52
Warren, Mrs. Otero, 8
Weaving, 2, 3, 5, 9, 12, 13, 14,
    15*, 18, 20, 21, 22*, 23, 25, 26*,
    31, 32, 33, 34*, 36, 40, 47, 47*,
    48*, 49, 53, 62*, 63*, 70*, 71*,
    72*, 74-79*, 80*
Woodwork, 9, 10*, 13, 14, 20, 21,

.

www.ingramcontent.com/pod-product-compliance
Lightning Source LLC
Chambersburg PA
CBHW032105080426
42733CB00006B/423